JANELLE KLANDER

COURAGE TO FIND *purpose*

STORIES OF FEELING LOST, OVERCOMING ANXIETY AND DISCOVERING INNER WISDOM

Thank you to my homies…
Josh, Jen, & Kat for always having my back.

Thank you to my family for all of your love and support, especially after I've set my mind to something you may not have understood. I've never questioned your love for me.

Thank you to all of the eyes I've had on my content and design. Your feedback was crucial support for me to keep going through this book journey.

Contents

This book may be for you if. . .

You're a seeker.

You feel like there's more to life.

You're ready to spread your wings.

You're anxious.

You're depressed.

You're feeling stuck.

You know you have gifts that aren't realized.

You know you have feelings that aren't being expressed.

You're ready to embrace your purpose.

You feel too much.

You're intuitive.

You want to be intuitive.

You're curious about your superpowers.

You're ready to go down the rabbit hole.

You're ready for transformation.

You're ready to step outside your comfort zone.

You're overwhelmed.

You're tapped out.

You know you have a unique purpose.

You're ready to live life with purpose.

You're craving freedom.

You're ready to step into your power like a total badass.

Introduction

At twenty-three, a strange feeling ignited inside me, a feeling that I was living someone else's life and an inclination to do something drastic. I had to escape everything I was doing and being. I had to do it now. Can you relate?

So I broke up with my boyfriend, quit my job, and moved to a country where I didn't speak the language and didn't know anyone to start a new chapter.

After spending almost two years traveling the world and living in Spain, I was unexpectedly brought back to Minnesota, back to the place I thought I'd escaped for good. This time, though, I lacked the certainty that filled me when I left. I was severely anxious and depressed. I questioned everything about who I was and what I was meant to be doing, and for the first time, I had an inkling that, maybe, I was meant for something great. Maybe, I had a greater purpose on this planet. Can you relate?

This questioning led me to discover that traditional methods of treating anxiety just didn't work for me. I knew there had to be a way to actually connect and heal and not just cope and mask my anxiety. Over the years, I've become obsessed with humans and how they evolve, how they can get stuck, and—most importantly—how they thrive. Now, I guide anxious, stuck professionals (just like I was) to live life with purpose and have fulfilling relationships, because if we don't have these things, are we truly living?

If you are like me, you get distracted easily and don't like too many rules. If so, you will be relieved to know this memoir isn't written chronologically, so you can jump around to whatever topic suits you. You'll be able to follow the story better if you read it from beginning to end, but each chapter stands on its own. In each chapter, I cover a different topic by sharing stories and insights from my journey, mostly from the last ten years. I felt called to write this book as a letter of sorts to that version of myself who needed to hear these stories from these perspectives at the perfect time.

I want you to feel two things while reading this book:

1. I want you to feel like you're not alone.
2. I want you to feel fucking inspired to live your life on purpose with purpose.

Take this book to the beach and read along with a friend. Read it when you need a recharge while you're at a festival. Cozy up on a cold winter's night and take it in. Share a relevant story with a friend who's going through something similar so they know they aren't alone and that there is hope.

If you align with what you've read so far, this book may have been written just for you.

XO *Janelle Klander*

CHAPTER 1

To Follow My Dreams

When I was twenty-two, I bought a book called *Delaying the Real World by Colleen Kinder*. In between applying to over 100 jobs (yes, seriously), I would comb through this book, running my fingers across its super smooth pages with excitement and guilt. (Guilt because I was supposed to get a "real job," not feel giddy about delaying it.)

Thinking it was a numbers game, I applied to more jobs than any of my friends. The more applications I submitted, I logically thought, the more chances I had. I didn't ever think to sit quietly and ask myself what I wanted, and what my heart desired. I didn't know that I could live a life that was in alignment with my soul's calling—I didn't even know that my soul had a plan (regardless of the number of applications I submitted, trying to do what I was supposed to do).

I loved my *Delaying the Real World* book and took it everywhere. I dreamed of adventures like teaching at a sports camp in Africa, teaching English in Korea, or biking through Central America. I felt alive as I read through these options, and I wanted to do them all. At first, I was excited to show people my adventure book.

"Look what I bought at the bookstore," I said with a huge smile on my face.

"Delaying the real world?" my friend said, reading the title like she was asking a question.

"Yeah, it has all sorts of jobs and adventures to take instead of getting a real job," I said proudly, but I started to feel kind of stupid showing friends my book as I was finally graduating with a Bachelor of Science.

This was the moment I'd waited for, the moment I'd been working toward for four years. It was also the moment my friends had worked hard for, so not surprisingly, they didn't get my fascination with "delaying" our hard-won goal.

• • •

I felt immense pressure from my father to get a corporate job that paid well. Because he worked at a clinic, he started making connections for me with pharmaceutical representatives, befriending them and asking if they'd talk to me about what they did and if they'd give me tips for getting into the industry.

I liked the idea of making a lot of money since, at that point, I was still a poor student. But I didn't like the idea of the job itself. After having coffee with some of these reps, though, I learned that they put in very few hours each week and some of them had side projects. Regardless, at the time I was looking for a job, most pharmaceutical companies had implemented a hiring freeze, so I wasn't getting that job post-graduation.

Still deep in job-search mode my senior year, I found information about a job in Duck, North Carolina in my adventure book that looked like it could be domestic enough to be okay with my parents (even though what I really wanted to do was backpack around Europe and explore places I hadn't had the chance to see during a recent spring-break trip to Germany and England). Something drew me to this position.

The job in Duck, North Carolina, was for a position working at a parasailing/pool-cleaning business for the summer. It offered housing for the workers and sounded similar to my time working at America's largest waterpark, Noah's Ark in Wisconsin Dells, where I spent the summer between my sophomore and junior year as a lifeguard with hundreds of people from all over the world. The job in North Carolina didn't sound fabulous, but I'd be working with other open-minded people for the summer and exploring another part of the country.

"It's not uncommon for the people working here to travel together afterwards with the money they saved," the owner told me, while having a very casual interview chat one day— that excited me. I felt my body open up to this possibility; I thought about where this could lead me. This could be the gateway to seeing the world and meeting other adventure seekers. None of those other boring, corporate jobs I was applying for excited me, but THIS did.

"I'm thinking about doing this summer job in North Carolina. It sounds similar to the setup I had working in Wisconsin Dells. I think it'll be fun and I don't have anything else lined up," I said one day to one of my closest friends from high school. She'd graduated college two years before me and was working for a big company in London. I'd visited her during my spring-break trip.

"I think it's silly to take a job making less than $15 an hour when you have a degree," she said, obviously not supporting my grand idea either, which filled me with shame. She was the one friend who I thought would get it; after all, she was adventurously living abroad and someone I looked up to.

"I heard you're moving to North Carolina this summer," a friend of a friend said to me. (I can't call this person a friend. She didn't seem to like me, yet we shared a mutual close friend.)

"I'm not sure I'm going yet, but I want to," I responded.

"I think it sounds cool, I'd do that," she said as she leaned in for more information on it.

As much I would have loved a friend to go with me, I didn't want her to go. We were merely acquaintances. She was the grumpiest person I knew at school, and yet, she was the ONLY one with a positive reaction to my idea.

. . .

My adventure book rarely left my side, and neither did my on-again, off-again boyfriend. We'd been together for over a year, and he had another semester to go. After that, he wanted to move in with me and, soon after, start a family. On one hand, the idea of that seemed nice, but on the other, I felt like vomiting with the thought of settling down with him, which seemed like a good indicator that it wasn't what I wanted.

I'd never experienced a connection like ours before. We were already practically living together since we spent every night together, worked out together, made meals together, and even had a couple classes together as we both were studying business administration. Being with him was the most fun I had ever had, but there was also a dark side to our relationship.

Every night out to the bar ended with him being angry at me no matter how hard I tried to make it better. This game exhausted me, and I broke up with him after a therapist told him he didn't have an anger problem. With only three months left of my senior year, though, we ended up getting right back together, remaining in relationship purgatory—acting like we were together, but knowing that it was long done.

When he caught me reading my book, I felt guilty, though I did share some things from my book with him because what if … what if he got over his anger issues and was just as much a freedom seeker as I was and we traveled the world together, getting along perfectly?

"I don't have the money to travel. I need to work after I graduate. That's what I came to school for," he said with an eye roll.

Silence was my only response as my "what-if" scenario of us being a romantic, adventurous couple died. He wasn't interested. He thought it was silly. My obsession with that book reminded him that we weren't going to be together in the future.

. . .

My father loves me deeply and cares more about my physical needs than anybody else in this world, but his attachment to how I'm supposed to be living this life has always left me feeling suffocated. Our interactions consist of him making sure my physical needs are met, while my emotional needs are starving for attention from him.

At the end of my senior year, I talked to my dad about my plans to work in North Carolina for the summer. Even as a college graduate, I still wanted my dad's approval, which seemed impossible if I wanted to start living a life that excited me.

"I'm thinking of going to work at this parasailing business for the summer. I don't have any other job lined up yet, and since it's just for the summer, I can keep looking for jobs," I said.

"That doesn't sound like a good option. You still have plenty of time to get a good job," my dad said, as guilt overtook my body. I knew I could eventually get this "good" job that was his dream for me, but I hated the idea of it.

"But, Dad, it'll be a fun summer job," I countered.

"You just went to college so that you could have a degree. You should use it," he responded.

The more I pondered the idea of moving away, the more I wanted to do it. I could almost taste the freedom I'd feel driving across the country into the unknown—away from my dad, away from my ex, away from the people who thought I needed a "good job."

"I'm going to do it, Dad," I told him.

"You can't! You won't have insurance. Your insurance ends in May. What if you get another hernia?" he asked.

The sound of screeching brakes echoed in my head. I hadn't thought of that.

I'd just had hernia surgery. Yes, in the midst of wrapping up classes, engaging in a relationship that was long over, applying for jobs, and reading my adventure book, I was also healing from hernia surgery. (Good thing my adventure book was small; I couldn't even carry a textbook to class.)

"Do you know how much it would cost if you had to pay for that surgery out of pocket?" he asked.

Had he finally found the one thing that could stop me from following through with this?

I had no idea how health insurance worked. I just knew mine ended the month I got my diploma and it was "good" insurance. I also knew I could get more "good" insurance if I got a "good" job like my dad suggested.

I had no idea if my hernia surgery would stick since it was the second time I'd had the surgery. I also had no idea it was actually an elective surgery—I would have been fine if something were to happen and I didn't have the surgery. I'd had the surgery because my dad said it was better to do it while I was on his insurance. I also didn't know that I could just buy my own insurance and pay for it out of pocket.

Talking to my dad filled me with fear of the worst-case scenario. His fear ignited my own. I decided I had to talk to the owner of the pool-cleaning/parasailing business.

"I can't take the job because I need to have health insurance. I just had surgery and I could easily damage it again," I told him, not even believing it myself.

There was a short pause.

"Ookaay," he said slowly.

I sensed that he knew that wasn't the actual reason I wasn't taking the job. It was as if he knew I was giving away my power to my father, that I wasn't ready to take control of my own life.

Hanging up the phone with the owner, I felt like my dreams were crushed, not because I really wanted to clean pools and help people parasail, but because my dream to explore and experience life felt like it was taken away. My soul was crushed because my body was saying YES to going to North Carolina.

What was wrong with me? Why didn't I want to get a good job like everybody else? A wave of shame washed over me for not doing it right. I felt lazy, wrong, and bad as my dad's voice saying "good job" rang in my head.

I wished that I could be like everyone else and just go along with what I was supposed to do. Why was I so obsessed with this book? I felt juvenile, stupid, and embarrassed for dreaming. I watched my other graduating friends apply for jobs and get hired right away, leaving me as the only one from my circle with no job.

So after graduation, filled with frustration, growing resentment, and now, depression, I moved in with my parents and continued my forceful mission to find this "good job."

•   •   •

Finally, I did it. After two months of applying for jobs, I was hired as a sales representative at a fuel card management branch for a third-party logistics company. Yes, it was just as fucking lame and boring as it sounds. Although I'd completed my mission and found a "good job," I didn't care to celebrate. The only thing about it that excited me was moving out of my parents' house. During the two months I lived there, I fell into a deep depression; I'm sure I wasn't great company for them.

Three months into my new job, I was already searching for my next adventure and lined up an interview to work at a Mexican resort. It didn't sound like I'd spend much time out of the resort. It sounded like I'd work hard and get paid less than I was making at my "good job," yet I yearned to break free from what I was currently doing.

So again, I was ready to do the damn thing. Still needing my dad's approval, though, I told him about my idea, and he quickly told me what he thought: it was ridiculous. Again, I felt stupid, shameful, and wrong for having the desires I had.

• • •

Five months later, I was at a new job, which happened to be next door to my old job. I was a representative for ITT Technical Institute, which, thankfully, no longer exists. After one conversation with a dad and his autistic son, I realized I could not morally work at this questionable private college. The kid ultimately wanted to be a chef and had no interest in our technology based programs. His dad wanted to give him the full experience of checking out his options. In the end, it was clear to me and his dad that this was not the right fit.

My manager thought otherwise. He was stressed out with the sales goals he was not making and was on my case for a week about it.

"You could have placed him in our IT program," he said.

"But he had zero interest in that program," I responded as my body contracted from frustration.

I was excited about guiding people to their dreams, but not manipulating them into a $90K degree that they will likely never finish and then be overwhelmed in the high interest rates. And after some time, I also learned that any credit earned there would probably not transfer to any respectable public university even though students were told otherwise.

Helping people work toward their dreams was exciting to me. It was one of the reasons why I took the job in the first place. It may have been a step-up from selling fuel card management systems, but it was not my dream job.

And the thing is, I was good at sales. In only a few months, I was a mere half point away from a promotion that none of my co-workers had achieved yet. But I wanted to sell to help people, not to force them into something that wasn't on their path.

This was the first time that I really understood the phrase "micromanagement," thanks to my boss. He should have been singing my praises for that work I accomplished, not criticizing every move I made.

I took a look at my co-workers surrounding me and I knew they were feeling just as suffocated and frustrated as I was, but they still showed up every day. I was there for a month and already I was desperate to leave.

I couldn't help but wonder. . . Would I ever be happy? Was I just hard to please? The idea of looking for a third job within nine months of graduation seemed ridiculous. I didn't even know what to apply for since I saw every job description as a prison sentence.

The hiring freeze at one of the pharmaceutical companies was finally lifted, but by this point I'd come to the conclusion that I couldn't morally work as a drug representative, so I turned down an interview for a coveted position and was soon dreaming of adventures again.

This time I took it seriously. I was intentional about every move I made. I went to the library on my lunch breaks and read books on living and working abroad. I combed through my adventure book once again and filled a notebook with research and possible plans. I began to feel grateful for my shitty job, because it was giving me the motivation to take the leap.

Soon, I felt confident about the idea of teaching English abroad. I knew I liked to work with people, and it was a job I could do anywhere. I picked out a TESOL certification program in Seville, Spain, and I felt excitement in my body just imagining it. I'd never been to Spain, but learning Spanish was on my bucket list. I thought I'd give it a go there, and if I didn't like it, I could move anywhere and teach English.

So there I was with another adventure plan and no one else knew about it. My plan was gaining momentum and I was gaining confidence around it by not sharing it with people who had opposed my dreams in the past.

Finally, I decided to share my idea with some co-workers. Thanks to our toxic work environment, they unequivocally supported my idea of getting the heck out of there. Most of them were older than me, so they encouraged my dreams like they were looking back on their own lives, wishing they'd lived with more adventure. They didn't know me well enough to have expectations about how I should live my life, and they didn't have emotional attachments to me that would require me to stay near them. They were my perfect cheerleading squad.

I soon picked out a flight, applied for a certification program to teach English, and started planning what I'd do with my stuff. I couldn't assume that my parents would store any of it as I had a pretty good idea that my dad would not be supportive of the idea.

I decided to tell my family in November that I was leaving at the New Year, giving them less than two months' notice, which I felt was fair. I told my dad right before he went deer hunting, figuring that he would take some time to process it in the quiet forest before reacting to something he couldn't change. I hated knowing that me living my life the way I wanted to live it was disappointing him, yet so much of the life I'd built was to please him. I'd only gotten my degree because he told me to do it. I don't remember ever asking myself if I even wanted to go to college. In the end, my father didn't take the news well, but my family decided to support me and to store my stuff, including my car.

The seven weeks leading up to my trip were exhilarating and terrifying. I had moments of doubt, sure, but those moments never lasted more than a few seconds. I'd held on to my vision for too long to let it go. Even though there was so much uncertainty about what it would be like, it felt real to me.

My mom, dad, and brother brought me to the airport the day I left for Europe. When I turned the corner after security and couldn't see my family anymore, it felt exhilarating, like I was separating myself from how they thought I should be living my life. I was creating space to understand who I was without their influence. I had two suitcases and no plans after my month of training in the south of Spain.

I finally had broken free from the "shoulds." As I waited for my flight, I experienced excitement and freedom on a completely new level as I was finally taking a step to live on my terms.

I still wonder what was there for me in Duck, North Carolina. Was there someone special there to meet? A lover? A best friend? Some opportunity? Some specific experience? I don't believe there is "one path." I didn't choose that path, yet I knew I was being called to it for some reason. I can say that with certainty because, looking back, my body was telling me my path, and when I didn't go, I felt a weird turning in my gut.

Boarding the red-eye flight from Minneapolis that night was the first big step in working my courage muscle, yet I still had a long way to go with building true bravery.

CHAPTER 2

Building Courage

"I am not afraid; I was born for this."

- Joan of Arc

As a seventeen-year-old Catholic gal, I had to take on a saint's name as my confirmation name. Many other people in my class chose a name similar to their own or the first saint's name they found, but I took it very seriously. I knew I'd know when I found the right one.

I took the time to read through as many female saints as I could find. I think I'd forgotten that Joan of Arc was even a saint, but when I read her familiar story—what she did and what she stood for—I felt inspired. I wanted to reflect the courage and faith embodied in her legacy. I knew in that moment "Joan" would be my confirmation name, and during my senior year of high school, I was confirmed as "Saint Joan of Arc."

I'd forgotten about this until I was thirty-three, and when I remembered, my journey and relationship to courage suddenly stood out in my mind. As you've learned, I haven't always felt courageous, yet it's been a big part of my personality that people recognize in me. It makes so much sense that I would choose someone like Joan to support my journey.

I've had an interesting relationship to fear. I've felt intense anxiety for most of my life, and yet I've also aggressively stood up to the things that scared me.

For instance, there was that time when I was eighteen and I noticed two men trying to break into our garage across the street from our house. Still wearing my light-blue pajamas with clouds and sheep on them, I grabbed the phone and ran out the front door.

Charging at them, I yelled, "What the fuck are you doing? Get the fuck off my property!"

The men ran off, obviously scared not only that someone had seen them but also of the intense vibe I brought at them. I didn't quit when they started running. I got into my car to follow them to see if I could find their car and see their plates. Unfortunately, I didn't find them on foot or find a car parked nearby so my chase ended there.

Although this act of aggression had an element of courage, it was mostly fueled by my own fear.

I drove back home with my hands shaking, wishing I would have just called 911 from my bedroom window.

Yes, I was bold. Yes, I spoke too loudly and sometimes too much, but it all came from my own insecurity. I lacked the courage to stand confidently in my truth. I lashed out from a place of fear, which appeared courageous, but it wasn't.

Planning and executing my adventure in Spain was the most courageous thing I'd ever done. That was the moment I chose to live my own life. For some reason, I thought I was behind everyone else, but now I can see the truth: at twenty-three, I was actually ahead of a lot of people, though choosing to live my own life meant that I was very uncomfortable.

I didn't tell you everything about when my family brought me to the airport. My dad was nervously walking ahead of me with my brother, while my mom stayed by my side, giving me emotional support while I vomited multiple times as I walked into the terminal. Yes, you read that right. I kept stopping at garbage cans to puke up the lunch we just ate. My dad and brother were totally oblivious, but my mom saw it all.

"Are you sure you want to do this?" Mom asked me.

"Yes!" I blurted out, wiping the puke from my mouth. I was

sick to my stomach that I was doing something my family didn't totally approve of, and now there was this grand moment when they had to watch me walk away from them like a scene in a dramatic TV show. It was definitely not my idea to have them see me off.

I was scared to walk away from them, but not because I thought I'd miss them. (I feel a little guilty admitting that I've never missed my family much. It could be because I haven't spent much time away from them, but whatever the reason, it just doesn't happen.)

Consider this: When I was four-years-old, I went to my friend's house to sleep over. The twins, Kristy and Tracy, were eighteen months older than me, and their mom was worried about how I'd do; they had other friends that were older than me that had to be taken home in the middle of the night. Understandably, she didn't want to deal with that, so she hesitated. Meanwhile, I was so excited to have my first sleepover and didn't understand why the adults were balking at the idea. I packed my little red suitcase and waved goodbye to my parents, never even asking about them while away.

So the truth is, I wasn't nervous to leave their side that day in the airport; I was scared of how my actions were affecting them and would affect them moving forward. I felt responsible for their feelings. I didn't want them to feel fear or sadness. I wanted to control things I simply could not control.

That day I was being stretched outside my comfort zone. I could have turned around and said, "This is too much, I want to go home." But I didn't. I didn't stop because it got hard. I kept going despite my fear. My desire for my dream was greater than my fear and I was starting to really feel the truth of that.

After an overnight flight and hours waiting in the train station in Madrid, I arrived in Seville the following evening. I'd booked a room in Cordoba, which I thought was at the edge of Seville or even part of Seville since "Sevilla" was my search term. In an exhausted haze, I went out to get a taxi. When I showed a taxi driver the address, he showed me on the map that it was actually about an hour and a half away. Insert facepalm. He didn't speak a word of English, and I barely spoke more than *hola* at this point. I was confused, but decided to trust that this Spanish dude would take me to the right place.

I arrived in Cordoba late in the evening, yet there were people everywhere. They were celebrating Three Kings Day, which is the day the three kings brought presents to all the good Spanish girls and boys (basically like Americans celebrating Santa on Christmas Eve). I had heard of the holiday, but I didn't realize I'd be arriving that day.

My driver stopped the cab and got out to talk to another taxi driver, and then those two talked to some police officers. He was telling them where I was staying, which was on top of the hill. The parade was blocking any traffic from getting there, and the celebration still had a couple hours to go. (I put this together through guessing as nothing was said to me in English.)

What were you thinking, Janelle? You're so stupid. Why didn't you look up where Cordoba was? I thought to myself.

Soon I was being waved over. They wanted me to get into a police car with my luggage with a nice-looking officer that spoke zero English. He attempted to speak Spanish with me a few times, but I just kept telling him I didn't understand as I smiled an uncomfortable smile. To my surprise, he drove me right into the parade.

For the first time since before I even left Minnesota, I smiled big and relaxed all the muscles that I'd just realized I'd been clenching. I rolled down the window and waved to all the excited children cheering. I pretended they were cheering for my arrival to Cordoba and to Spain. This shift of perspective changed my experience completely.

It was dark and the streets were lit up by streetlights and smiling faces. Kids were holding hands with their parents in anticipation of what was coming next. I remembered how I was in the middle of the celebration that centered around kids receiving presents and remembered my own excitement of that day as a child. They had dreamt about this night all year and I could suddenly feel the magick.

In that moment, I felt I'd finally arrived at my destination, and a wave of joy and gratitude came over me—not just for the extremely helpful Spaniards I'd met so far, but also because I'd been attempting to leave the Midwest for the past two years. I'd been building up the courage to speak my truth. I'd spent months researching and planning this move, and then I did it. And although I didn't understand where Cordoba was, it felt like I was exactly where I was supposed to be, in the center of a parade being escorted by a sexy Spanish police officer to my hotel on the top of the hill.

• • •

The big steps I had taken had landed me in Spain, yet I still felt pretty scared once in Europe. My first seven months living in Spain, I hadn't traveled much. I craved traveling outside of the country to explore new cultures, but I was waiting to find someone that wanted to join me. The few friends I had in Spain were either content with staying put or didn't have the resources to travel. It would take courage to travel on my own and courage takes time to grow.

Sure, I had hopped on a plane to Spain, but actually traveling alone felt like a very different thing. It was the next edge of my comfort zone.

I finally took my first solo trip during my first summer in Europe. I'd sent a handwritten letter to my relatives in Slovenia, and they responded via email. We arranged for me to visit them for a week in August, but beforehand, I'd stop in Barcelona to see a friend and then go to Venice—absolutely solo for the first time. From Venice, I'd make my way to Croatia for a week and then to Slovenia.

Honestly, Venice isn't the coolest place to travel solo. It's such a romanticized city that it really highlighted my feeling of being alone. I stayed at a campground outside the city and took a bus in during the day. Venice actually feels like an amusement park as it's not a city where people actually live anymore. I watched thousands of tourists take photos during its busiest month of the year and felt like I was in Disney World.

Although my solo adventures weren't that exciting in Venice, I did it. I failed at making friends after a couple attempts, but I navigated the city on my own and even felt confident doing it. I went where I wanted, when I wanted. I napped in a park in the midst of thousands of people. I ate pizza in a café . And even though I was never quite sure where I was, I never actually felt lost on the narrow, winding streets because I never really had a destination.

After three days in Venice, I waited for my boat to Croatia, my next adventure, and a country I knew very little about—except that my great-grandfather came from there. My grandma wouldn't give me much more information. She'd just say we were "*bohunk*" and that the borders had changed a lot over the years (she had one parent from Slovenia and one from Croatia). I grew up eating Slovenian foods, knew a couple words, and I knew the two countries had similarities—so much so that my great-grandparents had no problem marrying each other as new immigrants in northern Minnesota.

I had no plans for a place to stay in Croatia. My research taught me that the war in the 1990s destroyed much of the tourist industry, and it was difficult to find a reasonably priced place to stay among the little hotels with availability during peak times. I did learn that it's common for people to rent out rooms in their homes to make up for the tourists who still want to visit their beautiful country, so it left me to see what kind of room I could get upon arrival.

I took a seat on the boat near a handful of Australian men who looked about my age, and I enjoyed listening to their accents until everyone gradually fell to silence as it grew darker. As we got further away from the city of Venice, my trip suddenly felt more foreign to me. Even though I had never been to Venice before, I'd heard so much about it that it almost felt familiar to me. Now, I was heading into new territory, and I didn't know what to expect. I was beginning to feel more nervous.

When we finally arrived in Croatia, it was nearly 10pm and pretty dark. I was even more scared. What was I thinking? I'm a female in a foreign place, it's nighttime, and I have no place to stay. The voice of my paranoid father rang in my head.

Then, I felt some courage. "I am going to figure this out," I reassured myself.

Walking along the dock toward land, I struck up a conversation with one of the Aussie guys. They were friendly (I mean, I was a young woman, so why wouldn't they be?) and they said I was welcome to join them in finding a place to stay. Suddenly I felt less alone in the problem solving, and my entire nervous system relaxed.

Getting to know the five guys was fun. We found a fairly cheap apartment all together for the night, and the next day we rented a car and drove down the beautiful Croatian coast to the city of Split. I highly recommend this drive as the views are breathtaking. It was one of the most memorable moments in all my travels. The fact that none of it was planned made me feel even more present in my surroundings. I didn't know how long I'd be with these guys, but it was fun and I felt safe in the moment.

This part of my adventure opened up another level of confidence and freedom for me. I experienced what it was like to trust and figure things out.

The Aussies planned to make their way to the town of Split, so that became my plan too. When we arrived we piled into a new hostel with other backpackers from all over the world. I spent the next few days exploring the city with whoever in the hostel wanted to do the same thing as me.

And when I couldn't find someone to join me in whitewater rafting, I joined a group all by myself. From the outside it may have looked like no big deal, but deciding to do something like that solo was a big step for me.

I no longer felt like I needed to convince a friend to do the thing I wanted to do. I didn't need those unrealistic expectations for a travel buddy to meet all of my needs.

· · ·

The more things I did outside my comfort zone, every time I was thrown into situations that challenged me, the stronger this muscle became.

When I got stronger in this area, I was really just busting through some beliefs I had that were actually holding me back before.

For example:

"I can't travel alone."

"My dad won't approve."

"It will upset my dad if I do it."

"I'm responsible for other people's feelings."

"Foreign places are unsafe for me."

"I won't have fun if I go on vacation by myself."

"It'll be impossible to meet friends when traveling."

"I won't know what to do on my own."

"I'll get lost or confused if I'm alone."

"It's not safe for me to travel."

"What if I can't figure it out?"

It took work to see what those beliefs were. It took work to really see how they limited me. And it took work to see that they weren't true. (Or didn't matter. "My dad won't approve" - might be true, but forget him.)

Traveling was a great way to work my courage muscle. I had

learned I could handle anything thrown at me. Problem-solving became part of the fun on adventures. It felt so empowering to know that I could take a plane anywhere and find a place to stay, make new friends, and have eye-opening experiences.

I think back to when my 22-year-old self was begging her friends to join her on an after college adventure. She was willing to travel or move anywhere her friends wanted. She lacked the bravery to create her own freedom by walking on her own path.

The freedom to do the thing I desired was what I'd dreamed of—what my heart had yearned for—and now I have it.

To me, having courage isn't the absence of fear. It's about feeling fear and moving forward anyway. I've been called "bold," "courageous," "brave," and "valiente" more than anything else since I took that flight to Madrid.

When I chose Joan as my confirmation name, I was tapping into my purpose to inspire others to tap into their courage and step through their fears. It's taken me a while to learn to be brave, yet it's a big part of what people recognize in me now.

I've learned my bravery is always more powerful than my biggest fear and with this belief, I'm able to continue bursting through beliefs that hold me back, and show up like a badass.

CHAPTER 3

Pre-Awakening

For me there wasn't a single moment of awakening. Instead, it was an unfolding that started the night before I decided to make the big move to Europe.

I was lying on my back, staring at the ceiling, in a weird state of mind. (Now, I'd describe it as feeling connected to a higher power or purpose.) I stared so long, I started to feel like I was looking down at the life I'd created: Great boyfriend. Decent job. Nice home. Supportive family. Great friends. Physically healthy.

Yet I felt like something was missing.

Was I just ungrateful? In that moment of silence, I felt like I was staring off into another world, like I was disconnecting from what and who I was. What was I missing? I'd checked all the boxes I was supposed to in order to have a good life, but I wasn't happy.

Is this what adult life was supposed to be like? I felt like I'd been duped. I'd finally jumped through all the hoops and made it to adulthood, and turns out, it super sucks.

Then I had the realization: I was living someone else's life. I'd put together this life based on "shoulds" and others' expectations. I had few ideas about what I actually wanted. No wonder I was disappointed and longing for something more.

Ironically, I felt time start to speed up. Even though nothing was happening in that moment, a sense of urgency washed over me. I felt like if I didn't do something drastically different, I'd blink my eyes and it'd be ten years, thirty years, fifty years later. I saw flashes of what my life would be if I kept living as I was. I'd continue to be miserable and anxious.

And then something clicked. I had to find that thing I was missing, and I knew I had to do it by completely removing myself from this version of my life. I knew I had to create the adventure my heart had been longing for.

Well, you know what happened next. I dismantled my false life and started a new chapter.

I call that experience my "pre-awakening" because it was when I STARTED to open my mind and see myself differently. But it was only the precursor to my actual awakening.

• • •

I did some thrilling things while living abroad that looked great on social media. I took part in La Tomatina de Bunol (the world's largest tomato fight), attended some music festivals, visited my family in Slovenia and visited various cathedrals and castles around Europe.

"You're living the dream!" people would say to me.

I was living an adventurous life, sure, but there was more to it than that.

It wasn't all fun and games; I was being challenged constantly. I did my best to learn the language, but Spanish didn't magically fall into my brain from hearing it on the street like I'd imagined. I was starting from scratch so hearing a conversation on the street was just meaningless sound to me. Living abroad looks great on paper, but in reality it can be quite challenging.

Consider these mishaps: There was the time that I accidently paid forty euros to charge the wrong phone number and couldn't sufficiently explain my mistake to the phone worker in the store so I just walked away on the verge of tears. There was the time I found out my roommates had painted over the mold in my room right before I moved in, which explained why I started sleeping twelve hours a day and had no energy. There was the time I moved apartments and the landlord decided to keep my deposit without a valid reason. I wanted to say so much in these situations, but I couldn't. I was just left feeling powerless and frustrated.

I felt like I'd lost the power of my voice while living abroad. The fact was, I was speaking English all day at work, then I would hang out with my English speaking friends in the evening. Even though I was putting in some effort to practice Spanish, I had very little space to do so. I wasn't speaking at a level where I felt fully understood, where my intention was truly heard. And when conflicts arose, frustration would overwhelm me and I'd struggle to say anything at all.

When I would speak, I felt intense anxiety. I was terrified of making a mistake, and that fear doesn't support language improvement, because mistakes need to be made. My hesitation to speak was fueled by my lack of self-confidence, and it didn't help that the friends I'd surrounded myself with all were advanced Spanish speakers. I ended up relying on them as we navigated our way through the city.

I tried to make friends with Spaniards; really, I did. I met up with as many language exchange partners as I could. Most of them weren't serious about practicing English so we would meet for a couple of times, then they got busy. I did meet some cool people doing this, but none of them were really my friends.

At one point, I had the idea that I could live with an elderly woman to improve my Spanish and connect better with the culture. I asked around to my students to see if they had any or knew any lonely grandmas who wanted an American roommate, but the question seemed to come out a bit strange so I let that idea go.

Finally after six months of living there, I took a Spanish class in the summer while I had more space in my schedule. It was helpful and my Spanish improved, yet I still wasn't in any regular relationships with people to practice. And sitting in a classroom has always been my least favorite thing to do so I didn't return to take more classes after the summer.

I would get home from work and stare at my Spanish grammar book with dread. I was trying to learn this language in a way that did not align with my learning style, so it wasn't a surprise that I wasn't making big improvements.

At this point, though, I could answer all the basic questions a guy would ask me at a bar and knew how to ask for directions fairly well, among other things. But the fact remained: I lacked the ability to have an authentic connection in the language and that part was frustrating.

You may wonder about my dating life as that seems to be a great way to really learn a language and culture. There were no dating apps at this point besides Myspace, but there was this Spaniard named Santiago who I met in a bar one night. I learned that Santi's job was to guard the royal family on horseback. (Yes, seriously.) We dated for two months, but I broke things off because I just didn't want to lock myself into another relationship. Although I liked him, I didn't feel super excited about him. And that was the extent of my dating life in Spain.

When I was immersed at a bar or party, there were so many times when I wanted to make a joke but couldn't—or I'd try but it wouldn't translate. I felt like the boring girl in the corner who was quiet and had nothing interesting to say.

One time a new roommate had taken me under her wing and brought me out with her friends to drink on the streets of Madrid. It felt so fun and Spanish. I had longed for more connection with Spaniards. I could only understand a little and as the night went on, we all became more intoxicated. Soon I understood almost nothing.

"Do you understand?" she asked me in Spanish after she told a story as I smiled along with everyone else. It's not that I was pretending, but more following the vibe of the crowd.

"No," I responded and they all burst out in laughter.

I'm not saying that they didn't enjoy having me around, but my roommate moved out of our apartment the following week and we didn't hang out again.

. . .

Finding my way around the city was also an education as this was before smartphones were our navigators. I kept a pen and notepad in my pocket at all times so when I asked for directions, I would just stick my hand out because I'd likely not catch all of the directions anyway, so why not have them make a nice map for me.

I was constantly being sent to new locations for interviews or to teach a new class. Not only were the streets confusing (I really missed streets and avenues laid out in order of 1st, 2nd, and 3rd), but the first time I arrived at a building with my instructions, I was also totally thrown off by which floor the meeting was on. In Europe, the first floor is one floor above what we would consider the first floor in the United States.

Being immersed in this culture expanded my past beliefs about how things should be done. Even though there aren't as many cultural differences between Europe and the United States as there are between the United States and Asia or Africa, it still took some getting used to.

I was constantly comparing my culture to this new culture I was living in. When I traveled to neighboring countries, I compared those cultures too. It's like my mind was automatically creating Venn diagrams to help me understand how to categorize the new things coming at me.

Just a week into my arrival in Seville, I was surprised to hear a Spaniard took my friend to an hourly hotel to have sex because he lived with his parents. I was even more surprised to hear that this was normal as many Spaniards lived with their parents until they got married. I felt immensely grateful that this was not part of my culture. I wondered how many people had controlling parents like I did and married at an early age just to get relief and freedom. Seems plausible.

I know Americans are known for speaking loudly, but dang, Spaniards are not quiet people. When I first arrived I'd often get distracted by conversations I thought were heated arguments, but later learned Spaniards are just a passionate bunch who wave their hands around and raise their voices. Getting used to these Spaniards prepared me for my first visit to Italy, where passion was alive and well. Although, I'd have to say, Italians are much more forward with the ladies than Spaniards are.

There were many Chinese people living in Spain due to an agreement between China and Spain which allows people from either country to open businesses in the other. There were Chinese stores all over the city and were open all day, every day. This stood out because Spaniards close their businesses from

2pm to 5pm each day for lunch, or *siesta*, and they were closed completely on Sundays. When my friends and I wanted some wine on Sunday, we'd grab a box at one of the many Chinese stores.

I remember arriving fifteen minutes early to a business English class I had at a company, and the receptionist let me in the locked door with a confused look on her face. Arriving early is NOT expected in Spain. In fact, it's frowned upon—literally. This woman was frowning at me as she led me to the empty meeting room to wait. Arriving on time or being late is expected in Spain. I reprogrammed my internal world, my ingrained behaviors, to match that, something I constantly had to do to fit better into this culture.

I was realizing how much of my culture was just a framework of beliefs of how things should be done and while living abroad I would just have to do some reprogramming. Shifting my mind to match new ways of doing things wasn't easy. I did feel resistance as these mental beliefs made up the person I was and if I let them go, who would I be?

But in this process, I started to become aware of my mental world and the effect it had on my life. The uncomfortable shifting that occurred opened me up to see the world with more openness and compassion. I learned to see situations from many different perspectives, a trait that is empowering.

• • •

As I started living by different rules, I started to question who I was. I began to see that I'd felt some security in knowing how people saw me or labeled me in the past. One of those labels was "jock." I played three sports in high school and two sports my freshman year of college. In American culture, it's accepted for women to be jocks. In Spain, it's a different story. It's not that there aren't women athletes; it's just that women don't have the same opportunities to participate. When I shared that I played sports, people often looked surprised and then asked, "Really?"

"Yes, really," I would say, annoyed, as my ego was crushed.

I'd earned respect as a jock. My name was all over the local newspaper growing up. People knew me because of this, and now it was barely believable.

Some Spaniards would joke and say, "Were you a cheerleader?" Since they learned about cheerleading through American movies that made sense to them.

Because I didn't look like a typical American (as Spaniards saw Americans in the movies), many people assumed I was from Eastern Europe; specifically, they thought I was Romanian. On the street, Romanians would even come up to me and speak their language, and I would kindly say in Spanish that I wasn't Romanian. They'd just look at me in disbelief.

As much as my Spanish wasn't always grammatically perfect, my accent wasn't bad. I didn't sound Spanish, but I also didn't sound American either. (Thank gawd.)

I was even asked (multiple times) if I was a prostitute as many Romanian prostitutes hung out near the center of the city. So if I were walking down the street in that neighborhood, it wasn't uncommon for me to get asked, "How much?" At first, I was outraged. Then I began to confidently shake my finger back and forth, responding in Spanish, "Too much."

So here I was in a place where I had some new external labels, including "sex worker" and "cheerleader." But from another perspective, I had a clean slate. I had the opportunity to decide who I was going to be by letting go of any past identities.

No one around me knew who I used to be. No one was going to expect me to show up a certain way. I could be anyone.

I didn't know it then, but both letting go of the idea that I had to be something or someone in particular and trying on different perspectives are important parts of awakening. I felt the discomfort of my attachment to how I wanted people to see me, and I was starting to see beyond the physical identities I had carried. My mind expanded around how I saw myself and the world around me.

Letting go of a sense of security around my identities was both terrifying and liberating.

. . .

Just like my curiosity led me to Spain in the first place, the second summer there led me to leave for Thailand. After storing all my things in my friend's apartment, I headed to Asia with loose plans. I hadn't arranged any work for myself before leaving Spain, so I was open to opportunities while traveling.

It was just me and my backpack. My first stop was Turkey for a week. I stayed with a Turkish woman, about my age. It reminded me of my trip to Morocco less than two months prior. These two cultures were definitely different to anything I had ever experienced before.

I wasn't only getting curious about ways of doing everyday things I was witnessing in these cultures; I was also getting curious about religion and, specifically, spirituality.

When I got to Thailand, I kept seeing meditation flyers. I'd never meditated before and I didn't know anyone that had. I was fascinated by the idea. I even said to my friend, "Do you want to do one of these ten-day meditation retreats?"

"Ten days? That would take up too much of my vacation here. No," she responded.

Okay, so it never happened. But looking back, I'm proud of myself for being willing to dive into a retreat like that with zero experience. Something was calling for me. And at that time, I didn't quite realize how important mediation would eventually become for me—how much it would change my life for the better.

I started picking up books on Buddhism and spirituality while traveling around the country, and the more I read, the more curious I got. The more I opened up to other ways of thinking and doing, the more my mental structures appeared changeable.

This trip was a turning point for me for many reasons. My life was about to fall apart and I had no idea it was coming. There was no preparing for it; not even reading my spiritual books could have prepared me. And it needed to happen to get me where I am at today.

Up to this point, I'd experienced mental expansion, but I hadn't experienced spiritual or emotional expansion. A true awakening can't take place with just mental changes alone. We're so much more complex than that. I was teetering at the edge of a massive shift, not knowing what was next.

Everything in my life was about to change.

CHAPTER 4

Actual Awakening

I was sipping on a coconut smoothie, watching the Thai sunset, listening to Bob Marley's "Three Little Birds" in a small beach village. The song played every day like clockwork as the sun began to set. There was no electricity during the day, but it turned on just as the sun went down. It must have been the first track on the CD or however it was being played. The village was so small there wasn't even a road to get to other nearby villages. You have to take a boat or hike through the jungle. And there was only one Internet café to reach the outside world.

After five weeks of traveling around Thailand, I was exhausted. I got a scuba diving certification, trekked in the jungles outside of Chang Mai, ate massive amounts of Pad Thai, drank too much alcohol, met new friends every day, and was recovering from the "Full Moon Party" which takes place on a popular island not too far away.

Last Full Moon Party, I partied a bit too hard and after the sun came up the next day, I was standing in the ocean and noticed blood filling up the water around me. When I stepped back on the beach, I realized that I had stepped on a piece of glass in the water. I had to get six stitches at a nearby clinic, so I wasn't super mobile.

Settling in at this small beach village felt like the slow pace my body and mind craved. I hobbled around with my wrapped up foot, watching the rock climbers from all over the world climb the breathtaking rock formations. I took a kayak ride across the ocean bay and tried out a slackline for the first time.

I'd wake up in the morning with a huge smile on my face, because when I opened my eyes I'd remember I was in paradise. I wanted to stay past the date of my return flight and make this place my home.

I still had some money in savings, but since I didn't know my plans moving forward, I looked for ways to be thrifty. I asked the resort owners of where I was staying if I could trade English lessons for food each day if I lived there. They agreed.

I found a local who said he'd build me a treehouse to live in. "It'll take me one afternoon to build," he said, like it was no big deal.

This was from a guy I saw grab a poisonous black snake out of his hut and rip the snake apart with his bare hands without even wincing the day before. I knew he could handle the task.

"Wow, sweet," I responded. I had always loved treehouses and I had dreamed of having one since I was a kid. I thought this could be my chance.

So I began to really consider ditching my flight back to Spain and making this rugged little place my home for a while. I didn't feel drawn to go back to Spain, feeling like my time there had completed. The truth is I didn't feel entirely drawn to anything at this point, but I enjoyed where I was at.

This beach was really getting me to slow down and practice "being," which I was starting to realize was REALLY hard for me. I had been all about the "doing," but hadn't considered the art of "doing nothing" as something to attain. My injury, this quiet beach town, and my spiritual books were getting me to see the value of it.

Since I couldn't take part in most activities with my foot injury, I would just wake up, enjoy an outdoor shower, and have my breakfast along the ocean. I had nowhere to be and nothing to do. It was amazing.

. . .

Right now, you're probably ready to pack your bags and start your own adventure in hopes that it will solve your problems. Let me be clear: this was my path. You don't have to leave your life as abruptly as I did. When I was living in Spain and backpacking in Thailand:

My disconnection was still there.

My deep wounding was still there.

My unworthiness was still there.

My fear was still there.

And the worst part was, it wasn't even obvious to me.

I was still living mostly from my head. I was certainly drawn to leave my life for a reason, and I did start to feel more in alignment with myself as I traveled. But that alignment was so small. It was only a start.

Being abroad was amazing and filled my cup in many ways. The new scenery, crazy festivals, new friends, exotic places— they were all a beautiful distraction from my internal world. But I still had the feeling something was missing.

Adventure doesn't equal personal growth. I know there are many Instagram accounts that seem to tell us a different story.

Transformation can happen while traveling, sure. But true transformation often looks a lot messier than that. It can look like an unraveling, an unfolding, or a complete meltdown. And that was just around the corner for me.

. . .

While sinking into this idea of "being," I was also getting emails from my dad that were really killing my beach vibe.

"You have to come home. It's dangerous there," my dad said in one email.

He had heard of some people protesting the government during this time and was concerned something bad would happen to me while I was there, as he always did. I had seen some protestors the second week I was in Bangkok, but it was just a group of people wearing similar colored shirts and carrying signs. It didn't look dangerous and I hadn't heard or seen anything since then. Plus, I was miles away from Bangkok at this point.

My dad has worst-case-scenario thinking set into his inner program. I know it well, as it could be said I inherited it from him. It's not fun and can be quite overwhelming. My independence has always set off my dad's dark imagery of horrible things that could happen to me while traveling abroad.

This is exactly the reason why I hadn't told him about the trip to Morocco I had just gone on and why I had attempted to avoid telling him I was going to Turkey by myself on my way to Thailand. I had just traveled to Minnesota to visit my family before my trip to Turkey and Thailand. While there, I had used my parents' computer to print off my itinerary.

My dad found my itinerary lying in the printer.

My stomach sank when he told me he'd found it. From that moment, my dad's anxiety started to escalate. And six weeks later, it had amplified so much he became obsessed with getting me home.

"We need to get you home, Janelle. We'll pay for your flight," he said in one email.

It was bizarre to take those statements in when I kept describing myself as being in paradise, noticing the stark difference between my reality and my dad's projection.

I was angry and frustrated as the emails kept coming.

"You need to come home. I may not be able to work anymore. I'm sick and this will all get better if you just come home," he said in another email I read off of one of the four computers available in the village.

At this point, I was angry and confused. He was "sick" from worrying about me. It seemed unfair to ask me to come all the way home.

The thing that really got me, though, was that my mom and brother were being affected by this.

"I'm not sure what I'm going to do," I told a friend. "My dad wants me home for a while so he can settle down. It feels totally unfair."

"Yeah, I don't know," she responded.

How could any of my friends know what it was like? I hadn't met a person traveling whose parents wanted as much contact as my parents. Out of curiosity I would ask some people how often they speak to their parents while traveling. The answer was either never or once or twice.

Again, I hated that me living my life affected my family so much. I thought I had escaped it after moving to Spain, but turns out I couldn't escape it.

Apparently my dad's therapist had told him not to ask me to come home because it wasn't going to solve his problems. My traveling was just a trigger for him. I was grateful to hear that someone was speaking some logic to my family situation.

For years I was told by people that my dad worried because he loved me. I felt so agitated when I was told this. First, it showcases a toxic controlling behavior and labels it love. Second, I felt like I was the only one that could see how unhealthy it was for our relationship and that this act of "love" was actually creating distance in our connection.

The only relief in this situation was that now everyone could see I was right all of these years. I know my dad has always loved me. I also know my dad lives with intense fear, and that fear gets projected on me, his youngest child. My brother, who is four years older than me, has always had a very different relationship with him, but he's a man who doesn't travel much.

So unfortunately, the emails kept coming.

I had just paid for a more expensive summer flight to visit them for a month because I wasn't planning on being there for Christmas this year and now my dad was saying I needed to come back to stay with them.

I had a tough decision to make: Stay on paradise beach to live out my dreams or go home to respond to my dad's fear.

Guilt won when my mom finally stepped in and asked me to return. It was easier to say no to my dad, but when my mom asked, I felt responsible for fixing the upset my family was experiencing. Reluctantly, I took my flight back to Madrid and then eventually made my way back to Minneapolis.

As pissed as I was, I did hear a little voice inside me saying, "Go back for a while."

. . .

I returned to Minneapolis just as fall turned into winter. It was a shock to the system after getting used to the tropical humidity.

Arriving back felt. . .awkward.

First off, I'd developed a strange accent while being in Thailand—a mix of English and Irish with some Spanglish words sprinkled in. (Someone from Ireland actually approached me at the end of my trip to ask where I was from in Ireland.) I was shocked and confused by how I sounded. I hadn't been around many Americans, so I just kind of adapted to my environment. Suddenly, now that I was home, I had a hyperawareness of how I was speaking and how strange I sounded.

I'd spent most of the last two years comparing my own culture to other cultures, thinking about what I loved and hated about mine, and here I was back in the good ol' United States of America. I was living in my culture, looking at it with a completely new lens, and I'd brought back some judgment.

It was like I was relearning how to live in my homeland, which could possibly have gone more smoothly, but I didn't want to be living in my country. I had resistance to being back and this process of relearning. I missed Thailand and Spain.

Once (or twice) I pulled over on the side of the road in tears because almost every day I got lost in a city I used to know so well. (Again no smartphones.) I'd not only forgotten where things were, but I hesitated to remember significant names like Hennepin Avenue, Lake Street, Lagoon Avenue, and Lyndale Avenue. How could I have forgotten these well-known Minneapolis streets?

I couldn't exactly live my old life, but I was trying—mostly because I didn't know what else to do with myself. I reconnected with some friends, which typically involved drinking—happy hour, dinner, or dancing at a club. As much as I'd loved all of this before—even when I was in Spain—it was really starting to feel old. Something had started to shift when I was in Thailand, and I felt disconnected when I was in these situations. These were my only opportunities to be social, though, so because I didn't want to miss out, I played along.

I feel like I went through "reverse culture shock," but I think it's better described as a mind fuck. A total mind fuck.

• • •

Now that I was home, one thing I was excited about was dating. I'd barely dated while away, and I kind of missed

American men and was excited to be able to speak my native language with someone who understood it well. On top of the language barrier, dating also looks different around the world. In Spain, men will talk to women no matter their sobriety level, while American men typically don't make a move until they're drunk and it's near two in the morning.

Back in Minnesota, when I'd engage with men, they'd ask, "Where do you live?" and I'd reply, "I live with family temporarily." Or they'd ask, "What do you do?" and I'd have to say something like, "I don't know. I don't have a job right now," and I'd walk away feeling worthless, without a sense of meaning or purpose.

Even when I didn't like my job, at least I could say I had a job. I had a sense of duty and a way to contribute to society. I'd lost some of the labels I used to have, and I had no idea what to tell people I was doing with my life because I didn't know myself.

I wanted to move somewhere else as soon as possible, so I'd told my family I'd only stay through the holidays, making it hard to find a job for just a couple months. Would I get my own apartment or keep living with family? Would I continue to teach English abroad? Would I teach English in the U.S.? Should I just get a full-time corporate job and start saving for my next adventure?

I was overwhelmed and frustrated that I couldn't see a clear path for myself. I felt insecure that, at twenty-five years old, I didn't know what to tell people I was doing with my life.

. . .

I had a longtime close friend who had lived abroad and who I thought could relate to what I was experiencing. I was eager to see her, and, really, I just wanted to feel supported. I reached out a couple times, and when she didn't call me back, I finally directly asked if she was avoiding me because she didn't want to be friends anymore. She admitted that she didn't want to be friends, which felt like a blow to the stomach and sent me into a bit of a panic.

It didn't help that I was NOT getting along well with my parents, and although my brother graciously allowed me to live with him for a few months, he didn't have as much time to spend with me. I did connect with some other friends, but those relationships felt different too. In a nutshell, I wasn't feeling supported at a time I needed the most support.

As I looked around at my life, I realized that everything was different. I was different. And then suddenly, everything seemed darker. I stopped wanting to smile, and eventually I couldn't smile. I didn't see beauty in the world, and I couldn't remember if I'd ever been able to see it.

I disconnected from myself, and when I did feel connected, I felt overwhelmed by blame, shame, unworthiness, fear, and hopelessness.

I became adamant that my stay in Minnesota would be temporary. The days were dark and cold, and I was more connected with my negative emotions, deep insecurities, and traumas than I'd ever been in my entire life. I couldn't ignore what I was experiencing—depression and intense anxiety. I had to get out. But where would I go?

When I was living in a tropical paradise, it was easy for me to connect to the ease of life. It was easy for me to be positive. But winter shows us what needs our attention, not-so-gently highlighting the shadowy parts of ourselves that we tend to avoid the rest of the year. So there I was. . .in my darkest shadow.

• • •

As much as my mental and emotional state were affecting me, I felt just as affected by my physical state. I had migraines most of the time and an almost continuous sinus infection. I was immensely fatigued. I had irritable bowel syndrome. I had insomnia every night. I'd catch a fever or cold every week or two. I spent a lot of time attempting to manage my health, visiting various doctors, naturopaths, and other healthcare specialists. I ended up with a boatload of supplements, but my symptoms remained.

I kept going to more professionals who said they could heal me, but I still felt miserable. I figured I must be a hopeless cause. There obviously was no way to "fix" whatever I had because I was doing it all. Why wasn't my body functioning? Why couldn't I have one day where I felt healthy and energized? Why couldn't I have one day where I wasn't coughing up phlegm? Was it possible to go a day without having the nervous poos?

Months went by and I was still in Minnesota. I didn't feel stable enough to leave and the idea of it felt like escapism. I developed a belief that no one could help me, locking into my victim story of being damaged goods (the WORST thing someone can do, by the way). I kept telling people how miserable I was, attending health and wellness expos and going to booth after booth, telling my story of suffering. I was already doing so much of what was recommended. What else could it be?

Some suggested it was stress.

Sure, I was stressed (severely anxious, more accurately). But it wasn't until people suggested stress played a role in my health problems that I got more curious about the mind-body connection. Could it be the only thing that would heal my physical body was to heal my mind and emotions?

. . .

I'd hit a low point; you could call it "rock bottom," although I wasn't homeless, living on the street with a drug problem. Sure, my external circumstances could have been worse, but I felt like shit.

For me, coming back to the U.S. unexpectedly rocked my world. It broke my foundation and disrupted my adventurous life with freedom. It plopped me back in my old life with no identity or feeling of purpose. I had no sense of safety and little sense of worthiness.

Yet THIS was the best thing that could have happened to me.

When I was traveling, I lived more superficially, as my boat wasn't getting rocked too much. I could distract myself with new people and places. Yes, it was easy, but although I'd expanded my mind by cultivating courage and overcoming some limiting beliefs, there was still so much healing and growing that needed to happen under the surface.

I needed my world to fall apart in order to find my personal path.

When I interview people on my podcast, MOST of them talk about going through some tough stuff and feeling like there was no way out—but then they found a way out—and people are moved by these stories because they can relate. It's the human experience. It's not just talking about sparkly magic and positivity—most people can't relate to that shit. People relate to struggle, and when they hear about someone getting through to the other side, it gives them hope. If someone else can do it, maybe they can do it too.

For this reason, I'm grateful I left my tropical haven of relaxation to be thrown into the depths of my shadows. It totally sucked. It wasn't easy. But it was necessary. This was the beginning of MY awakening. Had I remained in an environment that didn't rock my boat, I might have put off the transformation that started to unfold when I took that flight back to Minneapolis. And to really understand this unfolding, I want to first give you a better understanding of my relationship with anxiety as my path to awakening has always been fueled by my desire to understand it and learn from it.

CHAPTER 5

Anxiety is Not Me

It's funny that, when I was in high school, my dad suggested I meditate to improve my athletic career. He didn't do it himself, but he'd read some athletes do it and it benefited them. And since he was the number one fan and unofficial coach of my athletic career, he wanted me to know. I had no interest in doing anything my dad advised; plus, it seemed boring. Of course, this was my teenage self talking. Looking back, I have a little regret for not jumping on this bandwagon at that age. No doubt it would have changed me.

During my basketball career, I noticed that I had a hard time breathing sometimes when I ran up and down the court. I told my dad, which then made it an official problem we needed to solve. He took me to the clinic, and although the doctor said I didn't have asthma, he gave me an inhaler anyway. (I'm still confused by this.) Looking back on this situation, it was clearly my anxiety becoming more intense when I played; I just didn't know how fear manifested in my body at that age. I wasn't even aware I had anxiety, but it was clearly there. I just thought it was normal stress.

• • •

At age twenty-two, I moved to Minneapolis after I finished college to start my adult life, thinking that since I no longer had to turn in assignments and take tests (since I was a grown-up), my "stress" would reduce significantly. It didn't, even though all I did was go to work and hang out with friends. I didn't understand what part of that brought me stress.

I still felt this slight panic about my life, just like I had always felt in school. At this point, I'd been in school for most of my life, so it was easy to just blame school. After all, what is this if it's not school stress?

Hmm, maybe I have anxiety, I thought, then I looked up the definition of anxiety and realized—Oh shit, I think this is me.

I read some clinical articles on it, and all of them said to talk to your doctor. I was due for my yearly exam with my gynecologist so I made an appointment and asked her about it.

"I think I have anxiety. I feel stressed all the time and I don't have anything to be stressed about," I said.

"Okay, do you want me to write you a prescription?" she responded immediately, without further questions.

"Sure," I said. Dang, that was easier than I thought it would be.

"I'll give you Paxil. It's for depression too. Depression and anxiety go hand in hand," she said.

"Okay, I've read that," I said, referring to the little web search I did prior to the appointment.

An hour later I had the little pack of pills in my hand. Could this really solve all my problems? Was this the magic pill I'd been waiting for? It was exciting to think it could be.

My doctor didn't give me any instructions, so I just read a few things on the label and took my first dose. The next morning, I took another dose. I felt a little tired but didn't think anything of it. Was it working? I wasn't sure.

That night I started to feel more disconnected from myself in ways I can only try to explain. I didn't want to watch TV because it felt like too much work. I just sat on my bed staring. My boyfriend at the time called me, and I looked at the phone with extreme apathy, watching it ring with zero reaction. I just lay there. Nothing in the world seemed important, not even speaking to a loved one.

The next morning I had to go to work because they expected me to show up. (I always went to work unless I felt very sick.) Completely lifeless, I got dressed and climbed into my car. My boyfriend called again. Again, I didn't answer. What would I even say? What was there to say about life?

My spark of life had been sucked out of me. When I was only about a mile away from the office, I pulled over, picked up my phone, and called in to work.

"I can't come in to work today. I'm not feeling well," I said with a completely monotone voice. Then I hung up and turned my car around, feeling next to nothing. I drove home and went back to just lying in bed, staring.

Everything in my life felt empty. I didn't see any point to living. It felt like the color in my life had leached out.

But I didn't feel anxious. Problem solved, right?

Lying on my bed, I remembered I'd started taking new medication. For a moment, I was able to step outside my situation enough to ponder, Hmm, I wonder if that's what's making me feel this way.

Although lifeless, the way I was feeling also felt very normal. It was my new normal, so it was hard to feel motivated to do anything about it.

I picked up the phone, though, and called the nurses' hotline on the bottle. I'm grateful I had enough strength and awareness to do that in the moment. I'd felt just a twinge of guilt for not going to work.

"I started taking Paxil and now I'm feeling very depressed," I told the nurse. "Like I'm not really living my life anymore."

"Okay, sounds like you should stop taking it," the nurse responded, sounding concerned. She asked me some more questions, and then we hung up.

The next day I went to work, and I started to FEEL again. I also started to feel my anxiety again, but feeling my anxiety seemed way better than what I'd just experienced. I apologized to my boyfriend for completely annoying him.

I later learned that depression and suicide can be side effects from taking Paxil. No one—including my doctor—had told me that. I started to think doctors didn't have all the answers like I'd previously believed.

And then I had this thought: If adults and doctors aren't what I think they are, maybe I should start thinking for myself more often, instead of assuming everyone else knows best.

My twenty-two-year-old self was gaining some confidence in thinking for herself.

. . .

So my anxiety was pretty bad when I lived in Spain, although some of my relationship stressors decreased because I wasn't managing expectations. I didn't realize how much anxiety was coming from my relationships—both friends and family—until they were gone. In some ways, though, my anxiety increased. Because I didn't have a support system, and was attempting to learn a new language and culture, I was living with a lot of fear.

When I was in Thailand, anxiety was definitely present for me. The truth is that no matter how yummy that coconut smoothie was or how bright the sun was shining, I couldn't outrun my intense fear.

After I moved back to the U.S., my normal rhythm of breath was short—really short. It was so shallow that I'd gotten used to yawning throughout the day, just to allow more oxygen into my brain. Even with that, though, I had headaches almost daily from a lack of oxygen.

I would openly describe my experience like someone was sitting on my chest or like I had a heavy weight on my chest. I felt like I was being suffocated all the time. It wasn't fun. And no matter how hard I tried to explain myself and what I was feeling to others, most people couldn't understand.

In addition to the physical symptoms, my thoughts were racing 24/7, and at night, I'd sit awake with them. Feeling the way I did—as though I had no control over what was happening in my body and my mind—was terrifying.

Fear had taken over my life. No: more accurately, I allowed fear to take over my life, and I was miserable. This was the worst my anxiety had ever been.

Since therapy is the normal protocol to support anxiety, I was ready to give it a go. I was feeling like I was ALL IN to heal myself at this point. I was ready to do anything it took. I had seen a therapist before—once in college to support me after a breakup and again right after college to support me with another breakup.

I walked to the cute office building at the edge of Uptown and Loring Park where many of the buildings are filled with therapists. As I walked in, I felt good that I was taking steps toward living a better life. I also was wondering if my anxiety was always this bad. I couldn't remember anymore.

Once I signed in for my appointment, I met two nice middle-aged women who told me I was going to take a test.

Sitting alone in a room, I took this test and answered the questions very honestly about how I felt each day or how I felt in certain situations. When I finished and handed it in, I felt a certain level of pride for being able to be so honest and for showing up for myself with true rawness.

After they looked over the test, the ladies sat down across from me, looking concerned.

One said, "Janelle, we don't understand how you can be so social."

The other one said, "You have severe anxiety for functioning in society as well as you do. It must take a lot of effort."

In that moment, the pride I had abandoned me. I felt disappointed, like there was something terribly wrong with me. I felt the struggle. I felt the fear of it never changing. I wondered if I'd been too honest on the test. Was everyone that honest on the test? In that moment, I didn't feel validated. I felt like I was deeply flawed and that my flaw was now being identified by these two mental-health professionals that didn't mention anything hopeful.

Yes, prior to this I'd known that I had severe anxiety, but having two therapists sit across from me with their concerned looks and labels seemed to make things worse.

I wanted to know that I wasn't alone with my struggle with anxiety. I wanted someone to relate to me. I didn't want to feel labeled. I wanted hope. I wanted to know that this wasn't who I really was.

. . .

Sometime after I met with those therapists, I went for a walk around the popular Lake Calhoun in Minneapolis with a close friend who was educated in family counseling and well-versed in common beliefs about mental illness. I was supposed to meet another friend after that meeting, and this friend wanted to walk around the lake one more time. Instead of just telling my friend that I had to go (a.k.a. creating a healthy boundary), I told her I was supposed to meet my other friend, expecting her to be "nice" enough to end our walk and create the boundary for me. She didn't. I walked around the lake feeling guilty for being late to meet my other friend and resentful of my friend for not picking up on what I actually wanted. (Exhausting, right?)

With each step I took, my anxiety got worse. My breaths grew shallower. I began to verbalize my frustration with having anxiety and that I wanted it to go away.

My friend looked at me and said, "Janelle, what if this anxiety is just a part of who you are? You'll probably always have it."

I wanted nothing more than for my anxiety to go away. I wasn't focused on being in a relationship, growing my career, a hobby, or being physically fit at this point. All I wanted in the world was to feel calm, to be able to explore a single moment. To be in the present. And my close friend who had studied mental illness just suggested that this may always be difficult for me.

In that moment, two things happened.

First, my breaths got shorter. The fear intensified, and terror filled my body.

Then a voice inside me said, "This anxiety is NOT you. You will NOT always have it," and my body filled with hope— replacing the terror that had just been there. I had hope that this wasn't who I really was at my core. I felt confident that I could find another way to free myself of my anxiety beyond what even professionals believed.

This feeling confused me at the time because I'd put this friend on a pedestal for knowing more about mental illness than me. It was the first moment that my truth started to come out—the truth about what this "mental illness" label actually meant to me.

I'd learned that when I ask for people's opinions, my reaction to those opinions teaches me my truth. (It's similar to what happens when I go to a psychic for life advice: depending on what they say, I either say, "Oh yes, I needed that confirmation," or "Nah, that doesn't feel right.")

That day at the lake I stepped further into my power, into my ability to identify my truth. I got the message from deep inside that I would not be ruled by anxiety my entire life. It was the message I was waiting to hear from others, but it was my truth. And it felt important to learn more about this freedom, not just for me, but for what the information can do for others as well.

(Visit www.janelleklander.com/freetraining for support with moving out of anxiety.)

CHAPTER 6

My Transformation

There was something that was just as important on my path at this time as trusting my inner guidance—being totally committed to my transformation.

And I mean totally committed.

I didn't want to feel stressed, anxious, or overwhelmed earlier in my life, but looking back I can see I let my excuses get in the way of making it a priority. It wasn't until things got really bad that I fully committed to myself and my transformation. Then something clicked, and I became willing to give everything I had to move toward my goal of being more present, to connect to a purpose-driven career, and to live a more fulfilling life.

I had always wanted to find a career I was passionate about, but being present and having more fulfillment in life was never a goal. Suddenly, all of this seemed urgent and important.

So there I was, with a very different perspective on my life. As much as I wanted to bolt out of Minnesota and live in Central America, I knew that I had to do this work.

Since I now had this new priority, my time and money had to reflect that. I learned that my priorities will always be what I spend my money and time on. I knew I'd have to INVEST in myself. Since I'd never invested time or money in this realm (besides a few therapy sessions that were mostly covered by insurance), it was outside my comfort zone and I didn't like being uncomfortable.

I wrote out a check to the first person I hired to guide me on my personal journey, and intense anxiety filled my body as I felt myself being stretched. I liked to be sure of things, yet investing in my internal world had no guarantees.

If I didn't have a guarantee, I questioned if my money would be better spent on that flight to Guatemala so I could relax and temporarily forget my problems.

But I knew I had to take chances that the average Joe wouldn't even consider because I didn't want to live an average life any longer.

I've always been more drawn to investing in experiences, but it felt like spending money on a trip to Guatemala was still "spending" vs. "investing." I had begun to accept that if I invested in my inner world, it would benefit me for the rest of my life.

To step into my greatness, I had to be willing to do things that were not convenient.

One of the things that wasn't convenient was meditation. My curiosity for meditation was still present after I returned from Thailand so I attended a couple group meditations and ultimately started meditating on my own each day. Although I enjoyed meditating in a group, I knew it wasn't realistic for me to sit with others every single day.

I know many people struggle with starting a daily meditation practice, mostly because there are a thousand excuses one could think of to not meditate at any given moment. But because I was totally committed, my thought process went like this: I have severe anxiety and there is evidence to back up meditation helping my anxiety. And even though I have never experienced it, I just feel drawn to it.

So just like that, I started meditating twenty minutes a day from there on out. I started out doing it in my car on my lunch break. I walked back to my toxic work environment feeling refreshed and less attached to any drama that would occur the second half the day. I started to question how I ever got through a workday without it. I realized the feeling I got after meditating was what I was searching for whenever I took a drink of alcohol.

That being said, meditation did not cure my anxiety. It helped it tremendously, but it did not make it go away completely. So I increased my meditation time, first to 1 hour a day, then to 2 hours a day.

I found that two hours a day was enough where I didn't feel "crazy"—meaning my head wasn't spinning out so I could experience some presence. Now you may think two hours a day is crazy in itself, but I'd often spent that much time watching TV or with a buzz from alcohol. My inner voice was suggesting meditation was better. And since just being in my skin felt uncomfortable at this time, I was willing to do whatever it took.

So I became curious about diving further into this perceived world of "spirituality," not connected to religion. I would go to the library and check out as many books as I could on personal growth and spirituality.

I was learning a lot. I felt like I had uncovered a whole new world that told me I could do anything. I felt inspired and wanted to share with a friend.

"Guess what I was reading today?" I shared.

"Another self-help book?" she said with a tone and eye roll.

In that moment, I felt distance between me and a friend that had been in my life for five years. The next moment I felt sadness and then acceptance in knowing that I had grown apart from her.

It wasn't a total surprise as we didn't have much in common any longer, especially since I had quit drinking. But if I couldn't connect with someone without drinking, I had to think—maybe our friendship wasn't that real to begin with.

It wasn't easy, but I knew it was necessary, so I let that friendship go. I created a new measurement for having and hanging out friends. If I felt excited about making plans with them, they were a keeper. If I felt dread or if it felt like a "should" to make plans, then they probably weren't a good fit for me any longer.

It seems obvious, but I realized I felt an obligation to see a few friends; what scared me was that obligation seemed normal. It was a rocky time for me, yet I had a deep knowing that I needed the people surrounding me to be my cheerleaders.

So I kept taking steps forward on my path, trusting that new people would come into my life. Between moments of "trusting," I was also terrified that my life was falling apart—because it kind of was.

In an attempt to take a big step forward with my growth, I bought a package to work with a hypnotist who seemed confident she could help me. If I'm honest, though, I didn't find her from my inner guidance, but from logic. Her office was less than a quarter of a mile away from my job and I thought it made sense to go to her as it was convenient. (And that was my mistake.)

I was obedient with what she instructed. I listened to the CD she gave me twice a day, sometimes more. But I really didn't feel much different after three sessions so I ended our work together, taking away the lesson that I needed to feel alignment with working with someone, not just convenience with location or cost.

· · ·

What I was feeling drawn to at this time was energy healing. I'd had a first experience with it back in Koh Phangan, Thailand when I was staying on that backpacker island, and it had made a profound impression on me.

One day, I'd found myself standing at the door of a healing center, looking at a menu of options. A traveler standing next to me suggested that Reiki was a good option if I had never experienced any of the healings before.

I was drawn to this talk of "healing" and "energy" so I decided to experience it for myself.

I paid for the session and before I knew it, I found myself lying on a wood floor while a Thai man made tones down my core and placed his hands on various parts of my body.

I was immediately relaxed. I remember thinking, "How could I be this relaxed after laying on a hard floor in a strange place within moments?"

Something was going on that I couldn't explain. My body felt fuzzy. I actually felt the energy move around me and within me like I had never felt before.

I was aware of everything that was happening. I felt like the session was finished at one point, but no one said anything to me so I stayed laying down. I had no idea how much time had passed.

Three hours later, they gave me a nudge and I walked out of the healing center in a fuzzy state. For the first time in my life, I felt solemn and peaceful. Words didn't seem necessary.

I just felt like being. I sat near the ocean for a few minutes, then remembered that my friend knew I left hours ago so I walked back to our bungalow in case she was worried about me.

She opened the door to our bungalow and I looked at her completely calm and emotionless. A dog had followed me home and sat alongside me facing her as she opened the door.

She had a surprised look on her face. She looked at me, then looked at the dog. Then she asked, "How did everything go? Did that dog follow you home?" She looked slightly confused.

I didn't know how to respond at the time. I didn't have words. Describing things didn't seem necessary. And I'm not sure how that dog got there.

I told her that I'd explain more tomorrow but I didn't feel

like talking much tonight.

She understood, but still looked confused.

"Your pupils are huge. Did you take drugs?"

A valid question.

I walked toward our bathroom and looked in the mirror. She was right, my pupils were big even in our well-lit bungalow.

"Yeah, you are right. Interesting," I responded.

I was a bit shocked myself, but didn't care too much. I just felt calm about everything in my life. Something amazing had happened during that session. I had released so much anxiety.

Strangely enough I had plans to attend a Muay Thai Boxing fight that night. I sat there watching guys beat the shit out of each other while I sat silently and peacefully.

The next day I felt it integrate more in my physical body so I was able to speak to other humans more smoothly. I finally felt grounded enough to share my experience with my friend. I also felt more joy, like maybe I hadn't experienced joy like that ever before.

The day after, I partied pretty hard at the Full Moon Party and ended up with that cut foot. I may have reversed those peaceful feelings with a couple days of hangovers.

That experience stayed with me, though, because I had never experienced that much presence in my life.

I had no idea what happened during that Reiki session, I just knew that something significant happened and I wanted more, even if I was skeptical as hell.

• • •

Back in Minneapolis, I had a strong curiosity about this energy stuff.

One year into my journey of self-discovery, I was meditating, doing affirmations, reading every book I could get my hands on, doing EFT. And although I had mini shifts here and there, I still woke up pretty anxious every day. I still woke up with a massive headache every day.

One day, I got pissed and I decided to pray.

I stood and spoke with conviction as tears streamed down my face, "You have to show me another way, there has to be more to life. There has to be another way. I know I am not meant to suffer. If I was put on earth just to suffer, I don't want to live this life anymore. But if there is more, you have to show me. I am ready."

I wiped the tears from my face and let myself calm down, then I stood up and I did something I had never done before. I took the bus downtown to explore a psychic expo.

I made a list of free classes I circled in the program that seemed interesting to me. I came in at the end of a class and decided to stay, even though I had planned to attend another talk during that time.

The class was highlighting an empowerment session that talked about spiritual DNA and more light. Honestly, I thought it all sounded pretty weird and I wasn't sure what "more light" meant anyway. I didn't necessarily feel interested in finding out, yet I noticed that I was still sitting in the room. I was listening to my inner knowing and stayed in my seat versus leaving where my head wanted to take me.

They announced that they would draw a name from the hat to choose for a free session as a demo in front of the group. I wrote down my name and threw it in. "Is this why I was brought here today?" I said with a chuckle. And in that moment, I knew they'd draw my name.

"Janelle Klander," they announced.

Unsurprised, I walked up to the front of the room and was the class guinea pig. The woman leading the demo kept asking what I was experiencing. Not going to lie, I didn't feel that much and was probably a pretty bad person to use in the demo because I wasn't going along with any prompts of things I should be feeling. Although I was open and seeking, I was also feeling quite skeptical.

But the days following that session, I noticed some deep shifts within me. It's hard to find words to explain it, but something opened up inside me.

I learned that the group doing the sessions were from a mystery school that taught ancient spiritual teachings that date back long before religions existed. I was intrigued.

I thought, "Maybe they can teach me some things that my self-help books can't."

And I was right.

I started studying fairly intensively with this mystery school— taking all the first level classes within those first 6 months. I really started to see the world differently, yet I was still searching for anxiety support.

I heard about a meditation course that lasted ten days called Vipassana, and without hesitation, I signed up for the next one. I had already been meditating daily, but had never meditated ten hours in a day. I was so curious.

After the ten days of meditating ten hours daily, I felt a little more grounded, but felt like I wanted something more. . . intense?

So six months later, I began following a three month protocol where I didn't watch tv, listen to music, or read anything that wasn't work-related. I didn't go to any parties and only hung out with one friend every once in a while.

I started meditating two hours a day the first month. The second month, I started meditating four hours each day and each week I eliminated more things in my diet. The last month I started meditating six hours a day, and ended meditating twelve hours a day. At this point I had a very limited diet of liquids. The last two months, I also did a daily martial arts routine working with the Qi (or energy) in my body. The last few days, I didn't consume any food and only drank water. Yep, it was the intensity I was searching for.

By the end of my three month journey, I had some incredible revelations and I had never felt so bright before.

Honestly, I didn't want to come back to normal life after it was over. I had grown to love my introverted life. It felt secure and cozy.

I had a mentor advising me during this process and I remember telling her, "I don't want to go back. I like it here."

She replied, "It's important to live in the light, but you also have to have your feet on the ground."

That response stood out to me over the years as I evolved and I still think of it.

I dove into life as a Healer, Teacher and Ritual Master. I committed further with my path as a purpose driven warrior and the school gave me the tools to make it happen. I did the prayers, rituals, and meditation I was told to do on a daily basis. I took it all very seriously because I took my purpose seriously. I dove into the inner workings of Kabbalah, alchemy, and ceremonial magick.

"I know you will use this, Janelle," my teacher said one day. It didn't stand out to me then, but I can now see that I was the student in class that ALWAYS used what I learned. It didn't make sense then, but I assumed everyone else in class was using what they learned too, but the truth was that many of them didn't.

I was all in with everything I did.

I became a healing practitioner for various modalities, including learning Jikiden Reiki. I began seeing clients and teaching meditation, empowerment, sacred geometry, and intuition development. Teaching these subjects seemed natural to me and I was excited to share because I felt connected to my experiences.

I met with a friend for years to exchange Jikiden Reiki on a weekly basis, which helped my anxiety immensely. Then one day, in the middle of the session, I got the message that came in a deep sense of knowing; it was time for me to teach that too. So I became a Jikiden Reiki Teacher from an institute in Japan and began certifying students.

. . .

My experience with personal growth was mental before I found the school. They supported me in learning to work with energy and power in ways I didn't know were possible which helped me to understand life and progression on a much deeper level.

My time in the mystery school was invaluable and it's hard for me to even fully explain my experience. But, as much as I appreciated finding the school, I knew it had an expiration date as there were some things that didn't align with my path.

In order to be a good student in the school, you had to do everything they said. I was on board to follow what they said when it came to using my tools. I was not aligned with their suggestions for how to enroll new people in the school, how to run my own healing business, or their suggestion to avoid working with other teachers and going to outside healers.

The structures of the school also didn't leave much room to have a negative emotion or space to repair any conflict with another member. I was told that if I had a negative emotion, it was my ego and my problem to deal with. I think because of this I also lacked deep connections with people in the school, as I believed that everyone was stuffing things down and pretending everything was fine.

I started to believe that being spiritual or living in alignment with my truest self wasn't just about fighting to obtain ego death or drowning in light. And, as far as I could tell, no one could outrun their humanness, so I wanted to learn to be a really fucking awesome human by learning the human lessons I came here to learn.

As my mentor said, "You have to have your feet on the ground."

My intention is always to live in alignment with my truest self and react to life less from ego, yet I didn't want to always be in combat with it. It was exhausting.

I wanted to learn to love myself fully—which included my ego—and to live with it. I still wanted to learn to be less reactive, but I could also see that my ego had some strengths that contributed to my purpose. I didn't hear anyone speaking about that in the mystery school or spirituality books.

First order of business was to not shame myself for having an ego. Man, that felt great. I already felt more powerful in just accepting that fact. Shame is the opposite of light, so I already felt more in alignment with my truest self by doing this.

Although I thought I had a good understanding of my own ego, I fell into a deeper understanding of what it was and its patterns, which opened up great power in me.

I then gave myself more permission to follow my curiosity

outside of the school. Not going to lie, it felt edgy, as I felt some programming around being "dark" or "bad" for learning outside of the school. But my path was also calling for it, and I needed to trust that.

There was so much that I learned from being connected to different communities. The things I observed among the people in the communities were just as valuable as what I was being taught. My intention was to be fully embodied when learning.

Something I wanted to learn more about was connection and communication. You'll learn more about my experience with this in the chapter on "Compassion & Acceptance' but in the midst of improving my communication skills, I realized I hadn't been that great at communicating in the past. When I looked around my spiritual communities, I realized I didn't see many people that modeled a great example of communication. Smiles, suppressing emotions, and then sudden outbursts of blame don't equate to authentic connection or solid relationships.

After these realizations I felt more embodied with my own personal growth. I studied nine years in the school and left knowing it was time. I knew I couldn't keep growing on my path and help people the way I was supposed to while still being part of the community. I don't think I've arrived at any destination of personal progression as I'm always learning and growing, but something really "clicked" for me with me with how I guide myself and others to keep expanding.

. . .

I remember one Thanksgiving when I spent the holiday by myself sitting in my living room, listening to music for hours. I had a smile on my face the entire afternoon and evening while gratitude exploded from my heart. I was beyond grateful in this blissed out state.

People often say they are chasing happiness, but it has never been my goal. By moving toward presence, fulfillment, and purpose, I've experienced more yummy joy and bliss than I even thought was possible. I've

It may sound extreme, but I never stop doing my work. I strongly believe that if we are not progressing, we are regressing. I've witnessed this within myself and others. I don't do this work out of lack or self judgement—oh, on the contrary.

I wake up and keep doing this work because I have self compassion and acceptance. And every bit of discipline and lifestyle change has brought me more freedom and love.

CHAPTER 7

My History with Drinking

Before my transformation, alcohol played a big role in my life. Like many people, it all started when I was a teenager.

My partying episodes from high school were few and far between. The most notable one was our basketball team's party (boys and girls teams), which was reported to the police. We were all busted. We were given a two week suspension by the state league and that was doubled to four weeks by our coach, which made playing in the playoffs impossible. All of the girls who attended ended up being kicked off the team. Although I'd attended a few parties before, after that incident, I was totally dedicated to my athletic career and didn't touch alcohol.

After high school, however, I was ready to party it up. During my freshman year in college, I started the habit of getting drunk on the weekend, unless I was playing an away basketball or softball game. Even then, though, we often partied when we got back if we weren't staying in a hotel.

The rest of my college career revolved around going out and getting drunk. When my grandma wrote me a letter and slipped in a $5 bill, that $5 bill would certainly be used to buy a red cup at the next keg party I attended. I don't think I ever missed class to drink, but it was my favorite thing to do on Thursday, Friday, and Saturday—and sometimes Wednesday and Sunday.

When I celebrated my twenty-first birthday, I wrote tallies on my arm for every shot or drink I had. I believe I got close to twenty. My roommate brought me to our apartment afterwards and panicked because I wasn't conscious—I was breathing, but far from conscious. She called 911 and the ambulance arrived. They left soon after they got there, but I was able to say the ambulance came to my house on my twenty-first birthday like some weird badge of honor.

My partying went on like this until I moved to Spain. Since some clubs stayed open all night, there was no rush to drink like I felt in the U.S. My partying actually slowed down a bit as I didn't have many friends who wanted to drink as much as me. But I did still party, and I still felt like I was missing something if a weekend night went by and I hadn't gone to a bar or touched a drink.

After I returned from my six-week trip to Thailand, I was tired. I'd drank a lot in Thailand—some might say too much. So now that I was questioning everything in my life, drinking was one of those things. I had to ask myself why I'd spent so much of my life drinking alcohol.

• • •

Each time I partied, when I drank my first drink, I'd start to get a buzz. I'd get that warm feeling in my chest—you know that feeling.

The anxiety in my body seemed to fade away. I had fewer inhibitions. I felt totally free to chat people up, dance, and be silly in ways I'd hold myself back in my sober world. I felt like I was unleashed when I was out with a drink in my hand. I felt more confident, more myself. I felt more connection when I was out than I did when I was sober. After all, it's easy to make a new friend while out drinking. You could have just met and suddenly they're sharing their life story with you in a bathroom stall, holding your purse while you pee. I didn't have that level of intimacy in my life, and it felt good to get close to someone, even if it was when we were drunk.

• • •

My hangovers have always been painful. I'm not sure I can even call them a normal hangover. I'd get an intense migraine that lasted the entire next day. My whole body hurt. Even if I had just one drink, I felt awful the next day. I tried everything under the sun aimed toward hangovers. Believe me. The only thing that ever made me feel better was an IV. I convinced a paramedic to administer one in his living room in Las Vegas during one vacation when I was twenty-two.

Then there were the couple times I woke up and realized I'd driven home. Those days usually shook me to my core; they were the worst-case scenarios of drinking and driving. It only happened a couple times, but it was enough to freak me out.

The more I started working on projects I was passionate about, the more I valued my time. A day after drinking suddenly felt like a wasted day that I didn't want to give up to the hangover gods. The more creative energy I tapped into in my life, the more purpose I felt. And just like that, I raised my standards regarding how I spent my time.

I also hated waking up the next morning feeling guilt or regret over some sort of misunderstanding I had with a friend.

Sometimes I'd clearly remember what happened; sometimes I had to piece it together. Communication isn't the most connective or kind when people drink, and a lot of it has to do with the inability to actually listen to what others are saying.

I also started to feel like the conversations I had while drinking were more and more empty. I craved a deeper, more real connection. I craved to feel inspired by the people around me, and I didn't feel that when I went out. I also wanted to be more INSPIRING and I didn't feel like I was very inspiring when I was out.

Since I'd started to shift my attention to my internal world of self-discovery, that meant my time and money were going toward these things as well. How could I justify spending so much money on drinking when my intention in life was to transform—and had I ever counted how much I spent on drinking in a month? It could add up quickly, but somehow it was always one of those necessary expenses where I looked the other way. I believed that I couldn't afford some things, yet there was always money for alcohol.

Now that I was perceiving the world differently, I was curious how I could gain new levels of freedom and calm WITHOUT drinking, and I wondered if it was even possible.

. . .

I went from being the friend who partied the hardest and the longest to the friend who was sober, which led me to ask myself, "Who am I if I don't drink?" I hadn't realized how much of my identity was tied up in alcohol. It had been part of my life consistently since I was eighteen, and now everything had flipped.

At twenty-six I still wanted to attend parties and go to concerts, so I did. But I was very uncomfortable in my body. At first, I wasn't sure what to do with my hands. Do I hold a glass of water? Do I cross my arms? Do I put one arm on my hip and one arm against this table next to me? Or is that too sassy?

Not drinking made me hyper aware of my body, and any awkwardness I felt or displayed around not drinking attracted more attention about me not drinking:

"Do you need a drink?"

"Why aren't you drinking?"

I'd immediately—and anxiously—respond that I didn't drink anymore, which some people saw as a game. They'd put on heavy peer pressure, trying to get me to have just one drink or just one shot. When I think about it, it's a little messed up that they didn't respect my boundaries, but I stood my ground. . .nervously.

It's fine being the only sober person at a party until the next level of alcohol hits and suddenly connection is nearly impossible. I'd feel the life slowly drawn out of me as I listened to my drunk friend repeat himself over and over again. I started to spend less time around alcohol and that wasn't always convenient.

Sure, I've felt like I was missing out when friends would gather to drink, and my last relationship might have gone better if I'd been a drinker. Yet I was done doing things to submit to my culture and to please others.

One Sunday afternoon I noticed a group of people laughing and dancing on the streets. I thought, that's so nice to see people just being that free. Then I realized it was St. Patrick's Day and those people were pretty drunk. Then I had the thought that it's rare to see someone letting loose, being silly, and dancing in our culture unless they're drunk. And if we see someone letting loose while they're sober, they're often labeled as weird or crazy. Something must be off about them, right? But if someone lets loose while drinking, it's totally accepted.

So I couldn't help but wonder, why can't we live in a world where we move our bodies the way we want to move our bodies, regardless of whether we drink or not? Why can't we be silly the way we were when we were kids?

Movement and silliness are so important to us, even as adults.

I love dancing. It was one of my favorite things about going to bars, and it was why I was all about the clubs. I didn't want to have to give up dancing because I was sober.

One night I was at First Avenue with a few friends for a concert and brought up the topic of dancing sober. Although I'd always loved dancing, I was used to doing it with a drink in my hand and with at least a little buzz.

"I dance sober sometimes," a friend said, confusing me. She drank ALL the time. The idea of her letting loose on the dance floor absolutely sober didn't seem accurate, but maybe I was missing something.

"I thought you normally drink when you go out?" I asked.

"Well, I do, but sometimes I'm sober."

Oh, okay. This was the first time I realized that people that drink have a very different definition of the word "sober." To some people, "sober" meant not drinking or taking any sort of substances that would alter their mind. To others, "sober" meant having only one drink or not enough to feel drunk, while to one of my other friends, "sober" meant everything up to blackout drunk. I'd never noticed the variation of meanings until I officially stopped drinking.

I took a deep breath and left my friend with her meaning of "sober" and walked downstairs toward the dance floor. That moment, making my way to the dance floor by myself without a drink in my hand, felt like a turning point. It felt like a significant step toward my freedom.

I stepped on the dance floor near where a small group of people were dancing, and I felt like I could feel what everyone else was feeling. And then there was me, overthinking, self-conscious, anxious, yet determined to have a mini breakthrough. I stood on the dance floor and started moving my body.

Dancing has always been a release for me, even when I was in middle school. I loved school dances. Of course I was sober then, although I didn't have the depression and anxiety that I now had, or the years of conditioning that connected dancing to alcohol.

In that moment, though, I danced. I let my anxieties pass through me and kept moving, allowing the dancing to heal me and bring me to a deeper level of freedom—one that wasn't connected to anything I needed to buy or put into my body. It's not like I was afraid of dancing sober, but at this point in my life, everything felt intense. I was slowly stepping outside the constructs of the reality I'd been living and it was scary.

• • •

I love being sober at social events now. I no longer carry that anxiousness I used to have, and I feel much more tuned in to whoever I'm connecting with. I feel tuned in to myself more—I know when it's time to drink water or when it's time to go home. I feel more in tune and grounded in my body to literally dance or move however I want. That in itself is a freaking breakthrough. That's the freedom I'd craved for years, especially when I was on the dance floor of First Avenue that night, awkwardly moving my sober body in the midst of strangers. An act that seemed so simple was a massive breakthrough, and I've been consistently experiencing new levels of freedom ever since.

At this point, no one even asks me about drinking. I'm so confident with not doing it, I don't attract that same attention, and I don't hang out in groups where it even matters.

I noticed that my podcast episode "How and Why I Quit Drinking" is one of my most played episodes. This really surprised me because I've learned that many people who enjoyed it still drink pretty heavily, which tells me people are curious about rethinking their relationship with alcohol.

CHAPTER 8

Losing My Religion

When I was in high school, I attended Catholic Heart Youth Camp, where I helped make improvements on people's houses. I didn't quite understand how teens who knew nothing about painting or house repairs were making a difference in the world through home improvements, but we had good intentions.

So there I was, painting an elderly woman's house. As I washed my brushes in her basement sink, there was a split in the wall in front of me where I could see a secret room that appeared to be a dungeon-like sex room for her middle-aged son who lived with her. When I walked around the corner to the next room, there was no door. And the other two sides of the room aligned with the edge of the house. There must have been a hidden door to enter. I went back to the laundry room to wash the brushes and to get another look. The walls were painted red and the only furniture was a double bed. There were some sex toys hanging on the walls and a box on the floor with more. I immediately felt uncomfortable with shame. I showed two other Catholic kids my discovery and we snickered with judgement. But truth be told, after the judgement passed, I felt some curiosity.

During camp, we sang Christian songs, which included "Our God Is an Awesome God." (If you know this song, you're probably doing the hand movements to it.) We also went to confession with one of the priests, something I'd done so many times before. When I was a child, I'd say to my parents, "I don't want to go. I don't know what to say!"

"Just say that sometimes you don't listen to your parents and that you fight with your brother," they'd respond.

Huh, I guess I do those "wrong" things, I thought, though at the time, they didn't seem that wrong. Like most families, my family was dysfunctional. And I was a kid, so sometimes I didn't want to listen to my parents. I loved my brother, but there were moments when I hated him.

So was I wrong because I'd done these things? This is where the "guilt" starts to set in as a young Catholic child; I was taught to "feel bad" for things I just wasn't sorry for.

As I sat on the metal folding chair at this youth camp, about to meet with a priest to confess my sins, guilt filled my body. I was older now— seventeen to be exact. My "sins" were bigger than not behaving in my family setting, although I still did that too.

Now I was having sex with my boyfriend.

Gasp!

It was a recent development. I'd been with Phil for eight months at that point, and he was my first for many things. I was seventeen and was in a relationship where I was loved and respected. And it didn't feel bad. It felt good. Except now I felt guilty because having sex before marriage was a big no-no in the Catholic Church. (I knew this before my mom started leaving abstinence pamphlets on my bed.)

It wasn't a rash decision to have sex. I'd thought about it for months, and I'd talked about it with him. I'd even made an appointment at Planned Parenthood, feeling panicked just parking outside the building.

"What if someone sees me? What would I say?"

This was one of the first big adult moves I'd made—deciding to have sex and seeing a nurse practitioner about it. I'm still actually pretty proud of myself.

I remember feeling so much anxiety while I was in the office. I wasn't entirely sure how sex even worked. Could I ask about that?

I didn't. I told them that I hadn't had sex and that I wanted to prepare myself before doing it. I had an exam. I got birth control pills and condoms.

I was ready for sex.

I remember feeling excited as I told Phil about my appointment. I remember feeling his excitement when he heard that I was now on birth control.

My first time having sex WAS special. It was also quick. And it hurt. But it felt right. Sexual energy is powerful and sacred. I felt grateful to share that with someone that loved me at such a young age.

But here I was now, on this cold metal folding chair, feeling guilty about something that was really special. I'm not sure if it came from all those Christian sing-alongs or if it was the shame surfacing from painting the garage with my Colorado friend who went on about birth control being evil. I didn't have friends who talked that way. In fact, I hadn't told any of my friends that I was having sex.

I started to feel like a fake Catholic. I felt like I needed to confess the truth. And that's what confession's for, right? So I walked up to this priest, who, thankfully, I didn't personally know. (I thought for a moment about what it would be like to go to confession with my priest at my own church where my mom was a church secretary. That wouldn't have been good.)

I nervously sat down and looked him in his eyes. I remember he asked me a question—whatever priests ask to get you to dish your evil baggage.

"Well … I have sex with my boyfriend?" I said, making it sound more like a question.

Part of me wished there were something in the Catholic religion that I'd missed—some exception to this rule where you COULD actually have sex with your boyfriend if it really felt right. I could tell from his reaction, though, that it was NOT okay to do.

His energy shifted immediately from having an open heart to scolding, which ended in clear instructions to do forty "Hail Marys" and forty "Our Fathers."

I stood up uncomfortably, turned around, and walked back to the folding chairs that were set up like a church congregation. When I sat down, I felt so much. I felt guilt, shame, and confusion.

Could the people around me see that he'd given me more prayers than them? Then I felt more confusion as I started to recite these prayers, which felt meaningless. This was supposed to cure me? Set me free? A part of me felt disconnected from the church, even though I desperately wanted to be part of it.

My dedication toward my religion continued throughout my

final year of high school, but I never went to confession again.

I no longer believed in it. It no longer felt right. My truth started to come out. I still wanted to be spiritual. I still wanted to be Catholic. At the time, it was the only spiritual option I knew.

I also continued to have sex with my boyfriend. And I continued to enjoy it.

• • •

Although I hadn't been to church in years, besides some Easters and Christmases, I referred to myself as Catholic, or *Católica*, when I was in Spain, because it felt like a way I could belong in a country where I was an outsider.

As I passed by the city churches with people pouring out of them, I wondered what it would like to attend a mass someday. My Spanish was getting better, but I had a feeling it would be hard to follow. On second thought, I wondered, does the format of a Catholic mass really change from country to country?

Probably not.

Ultimately, I didn't have any motivation to go as I didn't think it'd make me a better person. I didn't see that it made people better. The only thing tempting me to enter those church doors was to feel a sense of belonging.

After moving back to Minnesota, I didn't consider myself Catholic any longer. It was a label I was ready to drop. My first big stand was refusing to go to church for Christmas the year that my family had begged me to come home.

My mom worked as a church secretary while I was in high school and college, and she attended Bible study throughout the years. I consider her a devout Catholic, and we butted heads a bit about belief systems during this time. I was angry at religion— Catholicism and all other religions too. I felt this fury come up inside me as I remembered all the guilt and shame I'd carried my entire life based on belief systems that didn't make sense to me. As a way to process it, I had countless conversations about religion vs. spirituality with angsty new friends. Thankfully, there were always people around me that wanted to participate in conversations on this topic.

Then, after a couple years, I didn't feel angry anymore.

I see this as a process of healing with most people who leave religion. When I get an angsty new "spiritual" person who wants to talk about the difference between religion and spirituality, I smile and hear them out, but I don't have the same to give as them. I've made peace with it.

Ultimately, I see "spirituality" as a term that describes someone finding their path. Being Catholic was part of that for me, but a smaller part of it. To me spirituality doesn't even have to involve a focus on a higher power, but it does need to involve awareness, love, and seeking personal truth.

• • •

Last year, I was on a panel with other young people who were asked questions about spiritual paths and beliefs. It was put on by a few churches that had retreat centers that were curious about new ways to market to younger generations.

The four of us on the panel shared how we were raised and where we were now with our spiritual practice and beliefs. As the panel was coming to a close, an older, churchgoing man raised his hand and asked us, "Do you believe that you're sinners?"

A silent, awkward pause emerged.

My chest got tight when I heard this word. I was brought back to the shame and guilt I was brought up with as a child. I was brought back to the last time I was in confession, when I had to pretend to be sorry for things that I didn't think were bad.

"Because when I think of my sins, I just pray and wait for God to forgive me," he added, looking up at the sky with his hands in prayer position.

I knew I wanted to respond authentically, so I said, "I first cringed when I heard you ask this, yet then I realized that what you'd call a sin, I'd call part of my shadow self. Loving, accepting, and understanding my shadow is part of my daily spiritual practice. I believe that part of living a spiritual life is being able to forgive myself. I think God would want us to love and forgive ourselves, not wait for him to forgive us.

I looked up and saw the audience silently nod in an approving manner. They may not have thought or said it that way, but it appeared that it made sense to them.

Now I normally don't use the word "God" or "Him" (in reference to God) that much. Words can be limiting, and I have less and less attachment to which words I use. I think words can separate us, especially when we're talking about spiritual beliefs to which we're strongly attached.

The beliefs of religions default into righteousness and separation, and I think that's the opposite of what humanity needs right now. I cultivate compassion and understanding for people who use different words than me. As Macklemore says, "Whatever God you believe in, we come from the same one."

CHAPTER 9

Trusting Intuition

"I wish there was a GPS for my life."

This was my Facebook post in 2008 after abruptly moving back to Minnesota.

When I wrote that, I didn't actually think it was possible to follow some sort of inner guidance. I was feeling empty, alone, and a bit hopeless.

I was just starting to see the world differently. I was craving more direction in my life, knowing there had to be another way of living I just hadn't discovered yet. I also really wanted someone to tell me what to do next so I didn't feel so lost.

Should I leave the U.S. quickly? What country should I move to? What should I do for work? Should I even leave the U.S. at all?

I was about to learn that I did indeed have a GPS for my life and it had always been with me. It's just I'd mostly ignored it, which ignited my anxiety.

Remember when I applied for 100 jobs? My intuition was screaming for me to take that job in North Carolina, but since it didn't make logical sense to me (and definitely not to anyone else), I ignored it. I was desperate to base my decisions on the best logical solution, but the sound reason of applying to 100 jobs didn't get me one of those jobs because I didn't feel connected to any of them. I was forcing it.

• • •

I chose my first college based on logic alone: Coaches invited me to play basketball and softball, I got some scholarships and my dad told me it was the smartest option as I wasn't sure my grades were good enough to go to another college anyway. But because no part of me felt aligned with going to school there, I wrapped up my freshman year hating almost everything about my experience.

I independently chose to transfer to a new college at the beginning of my sophomore year. My dad gave me a million reasons why that was a poor decision, but I transferred anyway.

When choosing my college, I kept some things in mind: (1) it was at least three hours away from my hometown, (2) it had a 50/50 split between male and female versus most other campuses I visited, which had a much higher female-to-male student ratio, and (3) it focused on group projects and hands-on learning, with which I thought I'd do well. These reasons made sense to me, and on top of that, when I walked on campus, I felt like I belonged there.

This was probably the first time I really trusted myself over my parents to make a big decision, and I'm pretty dang proud of it. I remember saying goodbye to my parents and jumping into my compact car packed full of my things to make the three-and-a-half-hour drive to my new dorm room on my new campus. With the windows rolled down, I sang loudly with a big smile on my face almost the entire way.

Moving to Spain was obviously one of the boldest decisions I'd made following a "feeling" or pull in a certain direction, and I had some good reasons for moving to Spain too. As far as useful languages go for Americans, Spanish was it, and I'd been craving a return to Europe after my trip to Berlin and London two years prior. It just made sense to me, although it didn't always make sense to the people with whom I shared my plan.

They often asked me a handful of reasonable questions like:

Do you have a job lined up? Nope.

Will you be able to get a work visa? Doesn't sound like it.

Do you know anyone? Nope.

Do you speak the language? Nope.

Those answers never seemed to satisfy the person asking because many things didn't make sense, but it didn't matter to me. I was already starting to trust my instincts.

• • •

I know I had intuition earlier in life; I just didn't give it credibility unless it was screaming my name. For instance, once in middle school I was hanging out at a hotel with my friends. We got out of the hot tub and started walking to the pool. When I got to the pool, I turned around and looked back at the hot tub. It looked empty, yet I couldn't shake this sudden urge to walk the forty feet back to the hot tub. I began taking steps toward it, feeling a strange pull that didn't make any sense to me.

My friend yelled, "What are you doing?"

I looked back at her but didn't answer because I didn't know what to say. I wasn't sure what I was doing; I just knew I had to go back to that hot tub.

When I arrived, I saw a baby facedown in the water. I quickly scooped it out of the hot water and patted its back while it coughed out the water that had filled up its tiny lungs.

The baby was old enough to walk and must have snuck in there after we walked away. It didn't make any sense to go back and look as it appeared that the hot tub was empty. (I would have definitely been able to see an adult in the hot tub.)

Sometimes I think of that kid and wonder how that experience affects his life today. I have no way of reaching him; I don't even know his name. When I found his family, they snatched him away from me without even a thank-you. Yes, that's right. I saved a kid's life and never got thanked. I stood there in my swimming suit, shocked, staring at the mother's back as she carried her son away and my thirteen-year-old brain tried to analyze and process what had just happened

So I'd always had my intuition, but I hadn't always trusted it.

Because my deepest core wounding is around feeling unsafe, trust is especially hard for me. When I was at my worst, I felt like I lived on one planet and trust lived on another. Sure, I had a lack of trust of others, but on the deepest level, I lacked trust within myself. I didn't trust being in my body. I didn't trust the path I was taking or the decisions I was making. I certainly didn't trust my intuition. It wasn't grounded in anything real. It felt too risky, but I began to see that not trusting it was even riskier.

• • •

Post-Spain, I started a few different businesses, though I wasn't used to hiring people and managing projects. I made a lot of business decisions based on logic and left out an important piece of who I am—my intuition.

Based on the excitement I felt after discovering a ton of interesting things at health and wellness events, I decided to create a wellness expo. I poured my heart into that first year, but I knew I had to get someone else to manage it the following year. I'd created enough of a foundation for someone with good follow-through, a good network, and vision could step in and make it happen.

I interviewed two women for the position.

One was a fitness instructor who had experience running her own expo and had attended my expo the prior year.

The other one didn't have any event management experience and didn't have experience working in any aspect of wellness, yet she was eager.

When I spoke to the second woman, I felt my body expand and relax. I felt optimism, even though she had no experience. She sounded driven and focused when she spoke about the opportunity.

Regardless, I chose the first woman because my reasoning said, "Duh, Janelle, she's a perfect fit."

My gut, though, was saying, "This doesn't feel right."

I remember sending her the agreement to sign while my gut churned, a feeling I was doing my best to ignore. I reminded myself that she had all the qualities I was looking for and that hiring her made sense; she could surely expand my event from the year before.

A couple months into the planning process, I was getting concerned. Things didn't seem to be getting done like we'd agreed. I asked her about it, and she finally admitted that she really hadn't been working on it and that she was in the midst of a divorce. That sinking feeling came back in that moment, as if it were saying, "I told you so."

Final score:

Intuition – 1

Logic – 0

I use sound reasoning quite a bit to analyze and organize parts of any business project, so I don't want to disregard it. It's a significant piece of the puzzle. Clearly, though, it's not everything.

I had to reschedule my expo for six months later and took over managing it once again. It disrupted the momentum I'd created as I had to change the location and the date from the previous year.

In retrospect, everything about this expo was a learning experience, and one of those lessons was learning to trust my instincts with business decisions. That one situation catapulted me into listening more clearly and then practicing trust.

Like courage, it was a muscle I had to work daily. It didn't happen overnight, but with awareness and intention I expanded it. I started with small things, like following my instinct to leave early to work and then realizing on the way there that I needed gas. I used it when choosing roommates to live in my house. I allowed my intuition to lead me to trainings, coaches, and people I dated. I allowed it to lead me out of relationships and situations when my reasoning and attachments wanted me to stay.

• • •

I had reached a level of initiation in my spiritual training where they gave me a magick name. "This is exciting, what could it be?" I thought. I bent down to receive this initiation and was told my name: Ceres.

I had never heard of it before and felt curious. I walked out of the room into a side room to sit with it. I felt totally high on the light, kinda like taking acid, yet to be clear I had taken no acid. I sat there with my little piece of paper that said, "Ceres."

I closed my eyes and asked for information on her. I first scanned the globe, I could tell she was from a culture in Europe. I then saw a woman wearing a green dress standing in a field that looked like tall grass, taller than her. Her energy felt very loving and motherly. I wrote all of this down in my journal and then walked out into the hallway where everyone was sharing their magick names with each other.

"What's yours?" someone asked.

"Ceres, I'm not familiar with her." I said.

"Aw, that's the Roman goddess of harvest and motherhood," he responded.

Well, that makes sense. And that tall grass I saw her with, was wheat. Which is ironic because I don't eat wheat. But nonetheless, she is connected to wheat. I searched her name and found some google images with a similar image to what I saw in my meditation. I didn't just see her though, I really felt what she stood for.

. . .

So I had got pretty good at connecting to my intuition, but I have to admit, even when I was good, I wasn't perfect.

In the more recent past, I was splitting my time between San Francisco and Minneapolis and was in Minneapolis for a week to see some clients and celebrate my birthday. Two days before my birthday, I was invited to a friend's birthday party at a bouldering gym where I'd been working out for the last couple months. I hadn't seen these friends for a while, so it made sense for me to go; plus, I wanted to do some more bouldering.

As the evening got closer, I felt more tired and disconnected from myself. Lying on the couch, I wanted to cancel.

"I can't cancel," I thought, as guilt sank into the pit of my stomach.

I couldn't deny that I felt like crap, and I was also about to get my period. I called my boyfriend, hoping he would validate my feeling that I shouldn't go to this party. Unfortunately, he didn't answer, so I put down my phone, got off the couch, and started getting ready.

As I changed my clothes, an internal voice said, "Something bad's going to happen."

I paused to take it in. "What? That can't be right." I thought it was just my resistance to going. And then I heard it again. "Something bad's going to happen, like you're going to dislocate your shoulder."

I paused again. I'd had shoulder surgery eleven months ago, and my shoulder was feeling tight and strong. I'd done some bouldering, along with regular weightlifting, to strengthen it.

In my tired PMS haze, I dismissed this message and let my guilt over not being a good friend lead me to the party.

I got to the gym, excited to see people and to climb, but, honestly, I felt a bit out of place when I got there. I tried to connect with a few people, but I didn't feel connected. I climbed a little bit, but I didn't feel the same exciting thrill as I normally did. I just felt like I didn't know what to do with myself in a place that normally felt really familiar to me.

I walked over to where some people were gathered at the rock-climbing treadmill. It's like a treadmill except it's for climbing, so it stands vertically and rotates as you climb. It's not something I normally do, but I didn't know what else to do so I waited for my turn and grabbed the first peg. I turned my shoulder to reach up for the next peg, and then I went down screaming.

"Look at her arm," someone said, pointing at my disjointed limb as I lay on the mat.

Yes, I'd dislocated my shoulder again. Unfortunately, my shoulder can't pop back in quickly like it did when I was in my early twenties, so I made my way to the emergency room in excruciating pain to get my shoulder put back in place. (I've dislocated my shoulder many times in my life, and each time it gets worse.) Everything my shoulder surgery had fixed was now torn up.

I've had to do a lot of forgiveness work because I didn't listen to my own inner guidance, even when it was loud and clear. I'm not perfect at trusting, but I value it now more than ever. When I let go of attachments and trust it, things start to unfold and flow.

CHAPTER 10

In the Flow

The idea of letting my inner GPS lead me around town had piqued my interest after a friend told me about his experience. I was ready to try it for myself as I was learning that living more in connection to this "flow" was an important ingredient to thriving and living above average.

My plan was this: I was going to listen and take action based only on my instincts. The first time, I hopped on my bike and at each new block, I listened to see if I should turn left or right or go straight. It was a fun game that involved really tuning in to myself.

Before I knew it, I was standing outside an old friend's house. (There was a moment, right before I got there, when I thought, "I hope I'm not going there!") This friend had shut me out of her life, and I definitely had some unresolved issues with her. It appeared my intuition led me there to show me I had some work to do around it.

I didn't go inside, and maybe I could have. Standing in front of the home of someone who doesn't like me, though, I panicked. (I should also mention she'd "unfriended" me on Facebook and I didn't want to show up like a stalker by knocking on her door.) I didn't think about her much, but clearly I had something to let go of and forgive. So after that experience, I did more healing around that relationship.

The next time I did this, I biked down a street in my neighborhood where I'd never gone before and ended up in front of an industrial building that made me curious. I stopped. This felt like my destination, but I didn't know if I could even go inside. After a little bit of time, I biked away, but I was sure that was my destination.

The next day, my friend connected me to his friend that owned an art studio. I'd been looking for a place to host my first conscious dance event, and when I called his friend, he told me his address. It was the exact building where I'd stopped the day before, and suddenly it made sense. I ended up throwing a pretty cool dance event there a couple weeks later.

• • •

Some years ago, I traveled to Mexico by myself, and when I shared with others I was going, they asked me things like, "How are you getting to your hotel from the airport?"

"I don't know. I didn't book a hotel and I'll figure out transportation once I'm there," I responded.

Gasp. "You don't have transportation or a hotel lined up?" they asked.

"Nope."

I'd traveled enough at this point to learn what worked for me. The flow of meeting those Aussie dudes and driving down the coast of Croatia never would have happened if I hadn't surrendered my need for control. Traveling solo seemed so much easier now because I didn't have to come to an agreement with anyone but my own instincts.

When I arrived in Cancun, Mexico, I decided to take a bus to Playa del Carmen, which was super easy. I literally just walked across the airport following bus signs, thinking to myself, "It's strange that people thought this would be confusing."

When I arrived in Playa del Carmen, I was greeted by a Greek woman who said, "Do you have a place to stay tonight?"

"No," I responded.

"I'll bring you to a brand-new hostel," she said.

"That sounds great. Can I get a private room?" I asked.

"Yes, there are private rooms," she responded, and we chatted all the way back to the new hostel.

After I got settled there, I made my way to the beach. While sitting on the sand and taking in the rays, I noticed a guy sitting a little distance away from me. I felt this strong urge to go talk to him, but then I felt doubt. I wasn't even sure what I wanted to say to him. Maybe, "I feel like I'm supposed to talk to you?"

More doubts come up like, "I'm not even sure where he's from or what language he speaks. Will he think I'm hitting on him?"

I sat on my beach towel, resisting this pull to speak to this guy, until I finally gave up and headed back to the hostel before my skin got too red.

Sometime later, I saw him in my hostel. At this point, I went right up to him and said, "I saw you on the beach earlier," and our conversation just kind of flowed from there.

His name was Erwin, and he was a trainer for the Pittsburg Pirates. I told him I was on my way to an event later that week called Awesomeness Fest. He didn't seem necessarily interested, but when I finished the last day of the event, I couldn't help but think he was supposed to be there.

"I think you'd love Awesomeness Fest," I wrote to him afterwards. "Sign up on the website and you'll be notified about the next one!"

What stands out to me about meeting Erwin was that he was definitely meant to be part of that community. He did attend Awesomeness Fest the next year and has become the poster child for the community ever since. He's attended more events than I have and now we share a massive network of change makers from all over the world.

I think about how there's no way I would have found a place to stay if I would have tried to make plans beforehand, as it was too new to be listed on any websites. I also think about how I was getting the universal push to speak to him on the beach even before I saw him in the hostel. Clearly, we were supposed to connect.

This is a great example of how following my flow was an important part of HIS flow and life path. After this, it was clear that listening and trusting isn't just about me, sometimes I'll be used as a connector for someone else.

Another time I flew somewhere without plans was when I went to Thailand. I met someone on the plane who invited me to come along with him to a resort on the coast. And then I met a gal in the airport who invited me to come along with her. I went with the nice English gal and ended up traveling with her for a few days around Bangkok. Then I met some nice English lads and traveled with them for another five days.

I often don't realize how much I'm clinging to my need for control in everyday life. I wake up with to-dos and obligations that often take me out of my daily flow. My travel experiences have shown me that beautiful things fall into place when I tune in and surrender.

. . .

Now I want to be clear: I'm not a fatalist. I don't think there's only one wave to ride into our future. I see it more as surfing a wave, and if it goes down, we catch another and ride that one out. Each one's unique, each day brings a different current, and sometimes different waves will still lead us to the exact same place.

After my first week flowing with my new friends in Thailand, I had an actual plan—to meet my college friend in Bangkok on the backpacker haven of Koh-San Road—so I took the long bus ride from the islands back to the bustling city. Even though we had the intention of meeting, we really didn't have a plan about when and where. I stepped off my bus and started walking down the street. Before I knew it, my friend was standing in front of me.

"Well, this was easy," she said with a smile.

We were both making our way to the same Internet café at the exact same time. We were flowing with intention to find each other. The key to this is to hold onto what you want and be flexible about how it comes about.

• • •

I was curious about Burning Man soon after I heard about it in 2008, so I purchased a ticket with a friend in 2009, but decided that my time and energy would be better invested in personal growth since my mental and emotional health were rocky. Over the years, I connected with many Burners in Minneapolis and even attended a Regional Burn there. After a tough break up, I was ready to spread my wings and try some new things so I joined a camp and got my ticket in 2016.

While there, I created the intention to find love, and I did a ritual on the playa to set that into motion. I was finally ready to let go of my last relationship, which had ended exactly one year prior. I knew with 75,000 people there, I surely could attract a lover.

The next night I went out with my campmates to a party, but a friend and I just weren't feeling it. I knew people at this party and I was excited to find them, but it just didn't feel right. So we left and walked down the path to a stage where some DJs were getting ready to play.

"This doesn't feel right either," my friend said.

I agreed and we kept going until we found ourselves at the infamous Thunderdome where we watched the last few battles of the night. As everyone was clearing out, we looked at each other and said, "Now what?"

"Let's head into deep playa!"

If you aren't familiar, deep playa is the edge of the vast open area at Burning Man where you can be certain you'll find an art car bumping some tunes. . . and that's exactly what we found.

"Yeah, this is where we're supposed to be," I said.

We both smiled and started dancing. I looked around as I danced, feeling like I was going to be meeting someone. I took out my handicorn (unicorn hand puppet) and pretty soon a guy with a big smile on his face was standing in front of me staring at my unicorn.

"Hi!" he said.

That guy was Josh, and we ended up spending the rest of Burning Man together. We laughed and played like we were kids, and we even kept seeing each other after Burning Man. Josh has become a very important person in my life. Even though we aren't romantically together anymore, he's one of my closest friends, and I think about how we would have never connected if I wouldn't have been tuned into the flow of that night.

• • •

Another time, I was at a music festival and had lost all my friends. There was one guy in particular that I wanted to meet up with; we had a bit of a connection, and I wanted more time to explore the festival with him. I started to feel desperate and anxious to find him. It was so dark, and there were thousands of people. How could I possibly find him?

I didn't like this desperate feeling that had come over me. It reminded me of the times in my early twenties when I took shots and chased men in the bars. (I didn't always physically chase them, but I'd let myself get attached to a fantasy of one of them and then desperately try to strategize to make something happen.)

I didn't want to do that anymore, so I sat down to meditate near a tree in the midst of people coming in and out of the main stage area. After about twenty minutes, I started to feel calm and free from my attachments of finding this person. I mean, who knows if it was even the best thing?

Then I heard a voice say, "Let go."

I took a deep breath and stood up. I walked for about six minutes through a sea of people to the other side of the main stage. When I stopped, I looked over, and guess who was standing right next to me?

Yeah, the dude I was looking for. I chuckled to myself as I said, "Hi!"

I was caught up in my own suffering of attachment, and I almost missed out on the flow of the moment that led me directly to him. A highlight of my week was this beautiful, open-hearted connection with the dude I found that night.

Some years later, I found myself in a similar situation at yet another event. Earlier in the day, I'd enjoyed a short interaction with a guy, and I wanted to get to know him better.

The last night of the festival I made my way to the main stage area and noticed how exhausted I was. My tank felt like it was on empty, and I didn't want to dance or get close to the music. So I turned around, made myself a plate of food, and sat near a fire.

I remember thinking, "I don't need to chase anyone," and I just allowed myself to relax after a crazy day. I had the desire to connect with him without any expectation that I would.

Ten minutes later I noticed a guy sit down on the bench next to me. When he looked over, I saw that, yes, it was the guy I wanted to find. I said hello, and he looked surprised yet excited to see me. We went on to have a great conversation.

By this point, you may think that I possess magical powers of being a magnet to men that I want to bring into my life. I don't know, maybe I do. Or maybe I have just started to master that recipe of intention, surrender, listening, and trust.

• • •

When I think about my freshman year of college, my stomach churns and my muscles tighten. I remember walking on campus and not feeling a sense of belonging or a sense of direction or purpose. I can only remember feeling a sense of obligation to my community, my parents, my friends, and my coaches. I couldn't seem to find any sort of flow when I was there.

During my senior year of college, I had to disconnect some aspects of myself in order to sit at my desk and apply for those 100 jobs. Each time I hit "submit," I felt proud, doing the thing I thought I should be doing, but I also felt intense tightness in my stomach and chest because I didn't actually want any of those positions.

I realized that obligations or "shoulds" are huge roadblocks to my sense of flow. And my flow is essential to living a life that is authentic and fulfilling.

CHAPTER 11

Compassion and Acceptance

During my time in Thailand, I dove into books on Buddhism as I took long bus rides across the country and lay on the beautiful beaches. One thing that stood out to me about the teachings was that they included practical life lessons.

As I read books on Buddhism, the topic of compassion came up often. Compassion sounds nice, and really, who would be opposed to it on paper? Yoga teachers share insights about it with smiles on their faces. No one's going to openly speak up against compassion, right? I wondered what I can learn about compassion that I don't already know.

The truth is I hadn't ever thought about how compassion pertained to my life up until that point.

I remember my seventh grade teacher telling me I was a compassionate and mature person because I finished the writing prompt of "If I had one wish…" with "it would be world peace." I went on to explain why world peace was important from the perspective of a thirteen-year-old.

When I watched TV commercials asking for donations to feed starving children in Africa, I would feel my chest melt and tell my mom to donate.

Surely, this all meant that I had compassion.

• • •

After I returned home from Thailand, I walked into a Buddhist center in Minneapolis with a friend who was also curious about meditation. I remember the warmth of the space that had nothing to do with the temperature of the room, and I felt welcomed in a way I hadn't before.

To be clear, it's not like I walked in and thought, "This is my community. I belong here." I didn't feel that. BUT I felt welcomed, met, and accepted in a way I hadn't at any church. I didn't feel like anyone at the center was trying to convert me or persuade me; it just felt like the door was open to support me on my journey whenever that felt right.

Since it was all new to me, I went early to participate in the beginners' meditation, and before I knew it, I was meditating. A few minutes into the experience, a man in the room started breathing intensely, like he was doing some sort of breathwork. We didn't get any instruction on breathing in this way, so I was confused and distracted by what he was doing. With each breath he took, anger ignited in my body and I wanted to walk over to him and slap him in the back of the head. I peeked my eyes open a couple times, and it appeared other people were distracted too.

"He's ruining my whole meditation experience," I thought with resentment as my body clenched.

When the twenty minutes were finally up, I was relieved. I couldn't wait for this guy to get scolded. The teacher checked in with everyone in class about their experience, and a few people shared. Then the teacher mentioned that it wasn't necessary to force your breath during meditation.

"Yes! Finally, he's getting in trouble!" I thought as I looked over at my friend with a slight eye roll.

So this showed me it's easy for me to have compassion for those who are suffering, yet not so easy when I don't think they're suffering and I think they're doing something wrong. Clearly, these Buddhists did have something to teach me about having compassion for ALL people.

• • •

After spending a couple nights in San Marcos, Guatemala, I took a boat over to San Pedro on Lake Atitlan to start another week of Spanish lessons. There were way too many English speakers in San Marcos for me to improve my Spanish, so I made arrangements to check out the neighboring town. As I stepped off the boat with my backpack, a nice man greeted me, saying he wanted to give me a tour of the town for a small fee.

I agreed, handed him some Guatemalan quetzal, and started on the dirt road through the city. He was excited to share about his community, the arts, sports, and. . . his religion. He was Evangelical, which, at that point, I didn't understand very well, but I was open to hear whatever he had to say. It was a good opportunity to practice my Spanish, and gratefully, I understood everything.

I told him a bit about my life—specifically that I didn't drink alcohol anymore, but I did dance as much as I could.

"Dancing is evil. Evil spirits make us dance," he shared.

"Interesting. I don't believe that, but it's fine if you do," I responded.

He went on to lecture me about dancing and about how I

should also become Evangelical like him. At the end of the tour, he proposed we hang out for the night, as a date.

"Aren't you married?" I asked.

"Yes, but it's okay," he responded.

"No," I said and walked away.

I felt pretty judged by this guy. It didn't feel like he took a single moment to consider what it's like to be me. There was no meeting me where I was at; there was only his effort to convince me how I should be living my life. This made me think it's impossible to have true compassion for someone if you have an agenda to persuade them. It didn't feel great being on the receiving end of it and I wondered how many times I had done that to others.

The next day, I told my new private Spanish teacher all about my tour guide.

"That guy?" he responded. "I know him. He smokes, drinks, and cheats on his wife all the time."

"Really?" I said.

He also went on to tell me how Evangelicals came into the town and built churches to convert the Mayans in the area. Apparently, it worked.

I felt confused by hearing these contradictions. And I felt curious about what it was like to be him—to cheat on his wife, smoke, and drink all while knowing it goes against his religion, yet not appearing to be phased by it.

. . .

A few years later, I dated a guy named Brad who was unlike any other guy I'd ever dated. He was a severe alcoholic who would occasionally preach about Jesus after a few drinks as he used to be a devoted Evangelical. (Yes, this was the next Evangelical I came in contact with after my time in San Pedro.) He hadn't attended church in years, and at this point, his life revolved around working and drinking and sometimes drinking while working. (Did I mention his work involved driving?)

When Brad and I met in a bar one day, there was an instant attraction. I was sober, he was not sober, yet there was a magnetic pull neither of us could deny.

"There's something about you," he said, making it clear he normally dated blondes, which I am not. It was also clear that he'd been pretty promiscuous up until meeting me.

Before I knew it, I was accepting a new label Brad gave me as his "girlfriend" with part pleasure and part entertainment, knowing that whatever this was had an expiration date.

Brad didn't drink around me, which would mean he'd get

severe night sweats from withdrawals on the nights we did spend together. He didn't avoid drinking because of anything I said—I tiptoed around the topic of drinking as I knew it was a sensitive subject. It was my first time being in a relationship with an alcoholic, and it appeared he liked that I didn't drink.

After hearing some small remarks here and there from Brad, I put together that he was also homophobic. Every time this came up, I challenged what he was saying and attempted to convince him to change his attitude. I was never successful.

Brad's characteristics obviously did not match many qualities on my list of what I'm looking for in a man, so I didn't take the relationship that seriously. I couldn't deny I was drawn to him, though, and at this point in my journey, I was tuned in. I trusted where I was being guided.

I asked in prayer one day, "What am I learning from him?"

"Compassion and acceptance."

My friends didn't get it. They thought I was backpedaling. "You've done all this personal growth work," one of them said. "Why are you with someone like him?"

I don't feel like I'm above where the divine is leading me. I felt alignment being with him, and I had to trust the lessons I was supposed to learn.

In the past, I would have never stayed in a relationship with someone who was homophobic. I was against it as it felt unfair and unjust. I was never shy about speaking up about this in the past, yet here I was dating someone who thought being gay was unacceptable.

My normal reaction to homophobic comments was to attack, to argue, to get pissed and defend. But I remembered my lesson with him was to learn compassion and acceptance, so I started practicing it.

One day at the kitchen table, I decided to bring up the topic. I took a deep breath, opened my heart, and decided that this time, I wouldn't argue my point. I'd really listen. (Mind-blowing, right?)

He'd mentioned before that his dad was gay, and I was curious to learn more. I could tell he respected his dad, yet there was uneasiness around their relationship.

"When did your parents get divorced?" I asked.

"When I was in high school," he responded, going on to explain how hard it was for the family when his dad left his mom, especially since he left because he was gay.

Brad was a teenager when he saw his family fall apart. I thought about what it must have been like for him during that time; I imagined he felt embarrassed and confused. This happened in the '90s, so it likely wasn't seen as cool and progressive as it might have been if it had happened today.

I asked more questions.

When his mom was abandoned, she got angry and embarrassed, and she took it out on Brad, saying things like, "Are you gay too?"

Of course he developed a negative response to gays. He wanted his mother's love, like we all do. I imagined he felt like he had to oppose gay people so he could still be loved.

Suddenly there was a click. I felt like I really got him. I felt compassion for his experience.

"That must have been so confusing to have your mom accuse you of being gay. It was almost like you had to prove yourself to her in order for you to keep her love and acceptance," I said.

He nodded his head.

It all made sense now.

And honestly, I don't think he'd spent time thinking about it before. I don't think he had spoken any of this aloud before, because I don't think anyone ever asked and listened.

Something shifted in him after he shared that with me. I felt like something opened up when he had space to share without me giving my opinion. I think he learned something about himself.

It felt good to have no agenda in the conversation. I wasn't trying to persuade him. I just had an open heart and desire to get his world. It felt like I'd opened a new door to connecting, and it helped me feel the realness of how my agenda would stop the flow of a deeper connection in my relationships.

A week later happened to be Pride in Minneapolis, and when Sunday rolled around, he asked me to go to The Saloon block party, where at least 95 percent of the attendees were gay men. There were moments when he looked uncomfortable, yet he was okay. He showed up and I was by his side and we had a great time dancing.

I had a blast, surrounded by gay men with my (maybe not so) homophobic boyfriend.

When I put myself in Brad's shoes, I was open to accepting him, regardless of whether we agreed. It took strength that, to be honest, I know I wouldn't have had years ago. Old Janelle would have argued until she was blue in the face and put up a fight like the Evangelical man I met in Guatemala. But what would that have done?

I'm not gonna lie. Homophobia disgusts me on many levels, so why would I create a space for someone who judged people for being who they truly are?

The part of me that was disgusted by homophobes was also judging them. The older version of myself would have thought that my judgment was superior to his judgment, so that in my world, my judgment was needed to put him in his place. I came from a place of, "I know everything and this person is wrong." It came from my negative ego and not my truest self. It did not come from love and acceptance, and it created a lot of separation in my connections.

We could all be judged for something that someone else truly thought was horrible and wrong. ALL OF US.

At first, I felt no compassion or interest in knowing his story. I needed to be right. Being vulnerable in connection doesn't come easy, so it felt a little scary.

"If I'm vulnerable with this person, will that mean I'm agreeing with them? What if I walk away changed by the experience? Will they think that I think this is acceptable if I really listen?"

When I had that conversation with Brad, I changed; my perspective shifted. I truly did learn a deeper lesson on compassion and acceptance. I felt less judgmental toward those who were homophobic. I softened and started seeing new perspectives in life. It appeared that Brad changed from the conversation as well. So much can happen when we take down our armor, put our agendas aside, and deeply connect.

CHAPTER 12

Open-Hearted

E ver since I can remember, my grandma talked about her death. "That's really beautiful. You can wear that to my funeral," she said to my mother with a smile as my mother nervously laughed.

I'd like to say this only happened once, but I witnessed this a few times during childhood. She meant it, and who was I to tell her she shouldn't look forward to her passing? She was depressed for most of her life, and I think the idea of her death was a gentle way out. To her surprise, though, she outlived her husband and my other grandparents.

I'd joke with her, "God isn't done with you yet, Grandma. You must have some more lessons to learn." She looked at me for a moment and rolled her eyes while I laughed. She wasn't amused.

My grandma did have joy in her life. Her family was the

center of her world. Her home had a revolving door through which family members who truly cared about her came to visit, but underneath it all was deep suffering.

·   ·   ·

We developed a very spiritual relationship in the last chapter of her life. I'd allow her to talk openly about death and what she thought heaven was like. She was fascinated with books that described heaven and psychics who could connect with those who had passed. I'd walk her through meditations and do energy healing sessions for her.

She was so close to ninety so we'd all hoped she could make it just one more month, yet it was her time.

At the end, she was suffering greatly, and by the time my brother and I drove three hours to say our goodbyes, she wasn't conscious. They'd given her such a high dose of meds to help with pain that she couldn't even stay awake.

So there I was, sitting next to my grandma, my last grandparent, feeling sadness, yet a bit of happiness that she could finally go to the place she'd talked about for so long. I held her hands and feet, secretly doing Reiki healing on her as my family sat around her in shock and sadness. I knew I wanted to physically touch her as much as I could while she was alive as I knew it would help comfort her.

I was by her side through the night and most of the next day, going in and out of the room alongside a dozen other family members. I wanted to be as present as possible with her and to support her by sending her healing to ease her suffering. I wanted to be there for her in her transition.

· · ·

Before my grandma died, I'd never sat near someone's bedside during the hours leading up to their passing. There was something about the energy in that room I can't quite describe, but others who have been bedside for someone else seem to know what I'm talking about.

Being present with her during those final hours, I felt the power in our family surrounding her. I felt the miracle and the preciousness of life.

I felt like I was being taken through the different stages of her life, the eras she'd lived through, the changes she'd seen in this world. I felt it in my body and soul and saw images flash before me, and then I saw myself in her place. I imagined myself lying on my deathbed, surrounded by my family as my life played like a movie in front of me.

Then I felt a contraction in my heart, as if I were being shown I'd been living with a closed heart. Sure, I had a ton more awareness of myself and the people around me. I'd grown in ways I didn't know were possible. I had more freedom and bliss than I could have ever imagined, yet I was living with a closed heart in many ways.

• • •

At twenty-two, I ended my relationship with my college boyfriend, Daren, which brought me both relief and deep sadness. We'd spent most of the past year and a half doing almost everything together: eating meals, lifting weights, playing darts, playing pool, playing racquetball, attending classes, partying, and sleeping. And so much of our time together was spent in laughter and joy. I'd never had that much chemistry with someone, and now he was gone.

Moving forward, I used my relationship with Daren as a ruler, and no one seemed to come close to measuring up. So for nine years I had very few relationships, and the ones I did have ended after a couple months; only one made it to six months.

I regret nothing about being single for all those years. I believe it was necessary for my growth. What I was feeling by looking back was regret for not having my heart open to more people, regardless of whether I was in a romantic relationship.

I realized I only thought it was safe to really open my heart to someone with whom I was in a committed, romantic partnership. What about the rest of the people I see on a daily basis? Now, as I sat with my grandmother at the end of her life, I realized it was an impossible expectation to live by if I really wanted to live a fulfilling life, which by this point, was my main life goal.

Nine years after my relationship with Daren ended, I did meet someone who measured up while attending a Skrillex Concert at First Avenue. His name was Ozzy, and I allowed myself to be more open with him than I had with Daren. We spoke about the future we wanted together, and it was exciting and terrifying because I'd never felt that serious about someone before. It was terrifying because I was afraid of losing something that brought me a sense of security and was so special to me.

My worst fear came to fruition, though, when Ozzy abruptly broke up with me one and a half years into the relationship.

As I looked at my grandma, I was still mourning the loss of this amazing person who had been in my life just six months prior. I didn't want to repeat the same pattern of waiting for the idealized version of love in order to share intimacy with someone. I wanted to share intimacy, connection, and closeness with more people whether that be romantic or not.

At my core, I felt the fear of opening my heart as I didn't want to be rejected and abandoned again. I felt this lack of trust was stopping me from really receiving love and connection with the world, and if I kept doing what I was doing, I'd be taking my final breaths of this beautiful life having one big fat regret—living life with a closed heart.

"What would it be like to live with an open heart?" I wondered as I stared out the window of the hospital, still holding my grandma's feet. "Really having an open heart to those I meet?"

Whether it be with my aunts and uncles who surrounded me in that moment, or a stranger who would only be in my life for a fifteen-minute talk as we waited for the bus, or an old friend from high school who I still felt resentment toward, or a romantic connection at a festival with no certainty if I'd see them again.

I had to go deeper and really ask, "How can I love more fully? More deeply? More vulnerably?"

What was this crazy expectation I had that others were never going to disappoint me? Why did I believe that it was better to avoid closeness in an attempt to avoid being hurt? Was it better to close myself off completely than to never fully connect with the world? Why save my openness for one person when I could give it to the world every single moment of every single day?

Staring at my grandma at the end of her life, I also really understood nothing is certain. My grandma's life didn't necessarily play out the way she wanted. But sitting with her at the end, I felt a sense of honor for the gift that I got to call her my grandma in this journey we call life.

Maybe it was OK that the path she followed wasn't the path she would have designed. Even though I believe I have a strong sense of my path, maybe it's okay that there will always be uncertainty in life and there is no real way to plan for it.

Whether it was my own projection of my end-of-life regret, my grandma's own regret, or perhaps a collaboration of generational healing taking place—something deeply changed in me that day.

The air was palpable with grief as we surrounded this woman who was so significant in our lives. And that day as my grandma took her last breaths, I vowed to live life with an open heart—and I'd start putting it into practice right away.

•   •   •

A little over a year later, I was riding the BART(Bay Area Transit) to San Francisco from Walnut Creek when I looked across the train and noticed a young man spit a loogie on the floor.

Disgust came over me, and I raised one eyebrow and said, playfully and yet with some judgement, "Really, dude?"

Getting my attention lit him up, and he immediately came toward me and sat directly across from me.

"Well, okay," I thought. "I'm curious. What's this kid about?"

I quickly learned that his name was Chris and he was nineteen. There were moments when he seemed shy as he looked down as we talked, yet he was flirty—REALLY flirty—as he asked if he could go home with me almost immediately. I felt confused at first. How could he be hitting on me? I was so out of his age range. Then I caught myself with the ageist belief, thinking that it was totally possible for me to be attracted to someone fourteen years younger than me.

Old Janelle would have rolled her eyes and felt uncomfortable at this point. She wouldn't have been able to handle keeping a connection with a guy hitting on her when she wasn't interested. On some level she'd hate interactions where she was disappointing a guy by not being interested. She would have felt frustrated that he was even thinking bringing him home was an option. She would have felt unsafe being around someone who was kind of throwing himself at her. She would have contracted her energy and acted annoyed. But this new version of Janelle was too empowered for that shit.

. . .

I felt genuinely curious to understand Chris' world. What was it like to BE this person? What were his passions? I imagined his world was different, yet similar to mine. Sitting across from this stranger, I felt my heart open as I began to understand him. I made sure my body was directly facing him, even when I had twinges of avoidance.

"So where do you live?" I asked.

"I sleep on the BART," he replied.

I was surprised. "You sleep here?"

Chris was homeless, sleeping on the BART during the day, and then roaming the streets at night. That explained why he asked to go home with me. The streets of San Francisco are rough.

"I've seen intense stuff go down," he said, going on to explain that he moved here from Alaska last year and didn't have any friends he could trust. He'd also learned he couldn't trust people he met on the street.

"They're all out for the money," he said.

He'd been living with his uncle while working at McDonald's until he was fired. He liked that job, but after being fired, he and his uncle got into a disagreement. He left and had been living on the streets ever since.

"What would your dream life look like? Where would you go? What would you do?" I asked him.

He paused, like he'd never even thought of it before. Like he'd never considered the idea that he had a choice in his life circumstances.

"I'd play video games with you all day," he finally said with a flirty smile, nodding in my direction.

"Aw, that's sweet," I said. Obviously, he was in survival mode, still trying to go home with me, and, really, could I blame him?

For a moment, I imagined bringing him back to my apartment, to the space I shared with my friend, her partner, and their baby. As much as I wanted to help him, I knew I couldn't do that. So I sat across from this young man and told him I wanted him to have trustworthy friends, a job he enjoyed, and a roof over his head.

He asked if he could come home with me one more time.

With my heart wide open, I said, "No."

He looked frustrated. "Why were you asking me all of those questions then?"

"I want to understand you," I replied.

A few stops later, Chris got off the train.

I have no idea what kind of impression I left on him. Did he walk away just pissed from the experience? Did he walk away feeling a glimmer of hope that people cared about him? Or did our interaction ultimately not faze him?

I don't think this story is about some miraculous interaction I had with someone where I changed their life forever because I kept my heart open. He looked pretty bummed when he left me. I have no idea what he was feeling, AND as I'm constantly reminding myself, I'm not responsible for his feelings or anyone else's.

What I can take responsibility for is how I treat people; how I stay open, make eye contact, and genuinely want to understand the world around me.

．　．　．

I got home past midnight and was inspired to write a post on Facebook about my run-in with Chris. It didn't seem like an extraordinary experience, yet something about it felt special.

I wrote the post thinking not many people would see it because most of my Facebook friends are in the central time zone, and it was past 2:00 a.m. there on a weekday night. Right away, though, likes and comments started to pour in, and they didn't stop for the next week. What touched people about this story? I was so fascinated

Some people commented, "You changed his life!"

It may have had a positive impact on his life, but I don't know that for sure. It would be a lovely stroke to my own ego to think so. I don't feel that this was what actually moved people, though.

I ended the post with, "Do you open your heart to those you meet?" This was the question I'd been reflecting on since my grandma's passing, and it appeared people realized by reading the post that they wouldn't have stayed open to this person. They would have shut down and avoided him out of fear—the dreaded fear, specifically, lack of trust! A great way to close your heart to the world.

"I would have felt unsafe with him," someone said.

So I had to analyze this further. By opening up to Chris, was I really putting myself in danger? Would avoiding eye contact have kept me safe? Would intentionally closing my heart to this homeless kid have made a difference? Would ignoring him have been the safest move?

This person wasn't much bigger than me. We were surrounded by people on the BART. I didn't feel in danger, but old Janelle would have felt unsafe, so what's that about? I don't believe that it's really about trusting the other person.

I wasn't in danger. At this point in my life, I was confident in myself. I felt grounded. I was able to tune into my intuition, which I've learned to trust more than anything with warning signs.

So why are so many people unwilling to open their hearts out of fear of getting hurt by others? What I really think is happening is a lack of trust within ourselves. Lack of trust in our own boundaries can create this feeling of unsafety.

For example, if I looked this person in the eyes, would I then feel obligated to take him home with me? I have to admit, I did feel a bit guilty for not taking him home. I did feel guilty for not saving him from homelessness or giving him some money from my wallet.

So maybe these people thought they'd feel so guilty they would have felt like they HAD to do something in order to be a good person.

At this point, I'd cultivated some trust in my boundaries. Even with some guilt, I mostly felt okay telling this person no when he asked (multiple times) to stay at my home that night because I knew I could say that and still have my heart open.

I get it. I've had my guard up most of my life, but as I realized from the day my grandma passed, it really hasn't served me well. This experience felt significant to me because it's shown me how much I've grown into the woman I am today.

It's not always comfortable to keep my heart open—I'd say it even takes courage—but I can say it's worth it.

CHAPTER 13

I'm not for everyone

I don't remember the exact moment I chose the name *Badass Spiritual Warriors* for my podcast. After I decided to create a podcast, I just knew that was the name. It embodied everything I stood for, and I imagined the words would click with my audience. I felt excited about putting myself out there in a way that felt really authentic.

Although I'd had many other logos created in the past, for the first time what I wanted felt really specific. I hired a few different designers before getting it just right. At first, all of this planning felt fun; then it got closer to launch, and doubts filled my head, especially when it came to the name.

"What am I doing? This name will offend people."

And I wasn't sure of the latest status of "badass." Was it a swear word? Was it not? It wouldn't offend my people, but it certainly would offend others. I thought of some family members that might be offended.

Then it hit me: "Why would I want to please people that weren't my people?"

I took a deep breath in and realized I was about to start a journey during which I'd offend more people than if I held back, played small, and didn't release my podcast. BUT I knew that it'd be worth it to be able to live my truth every day. And by living my truth, I'd inspire MY people, just how I saw my life purpose laying out.

• • •

After the first big hurdle of doubts (believe me, there were many), I reached out to a young woman with a nicely followed YouTube channel. I'd found a video of her talking about self-love, and even though most of her videos were on beauty, I thought she'd be a good fit for my podcast. So I wrote her a message, introducing myself and asking her if she wanted to be a guest on my show.

To my surprise I got this message back:

Hello. Thank you for the offer. To be honest, I'm not a fan of my name being on websites or anything with lots of cursing. I will be having children and a family one day and personally would like to keep my name professional. Thank you for the offer though. Good luck!

Best,

Ashley

This was my response:

Hey Ashley, I just want to make sure I understand you. . ."bad-ass" is cursing? Or is there something else that I'm missing?

Her response:

To me, I would say so. Your website is where I saw it.

So there I had it. I'd met my first person that was NOT into the name of my podcast, just like I'd anticipated. Her reaction made it clear she didn't get what I was up to, therefore she wouldn't have been a good fit for my podcast anyway.

I felt misunderstood by her, but guess what? I was okay. I felt like she and I were living in different worlds. Maybe neither one of us could really understand each other, and that was okay.

After that experience, something shifted. I'm not saying negative feedback doesn't affect me, but I am saying that it doesn't faze me like it used to. I started to see people not liking what I was doing as a good thing. I knew I was doing something right if I had some haters because if I didn't, it probably meant I was being too general, trying to please too many people, and that I wasn't fully showing up as myself in this world.

• • •

For a while I was creating monthly events that were aimed at having authentic, unscripted conversations about various topics. I asked three people to be on my panel at each event, then facilitated a discussion for the audience. I had covered some topics like awakening, self-love, and relationships, and felt drawn to have a discussion about men, especially how men were raised, conditioning that happens, and repression of emotions. At the time, I felt like it was an overlooked topic that affects so many other issues our society faces.

I wasn't sure where the conversation would go (and keep in mind this was before the #MeToo movement), but I just felt called to create this event at that moment in time. I wasn't entirely sure what to call it since it was general, but I decided to go with "Manhood."

After creating the online event, I put it out to the world of Facebook, and shortly after, I got a message from an acquaintance. She said that she and another woman were triggered by the name of my event.

"When are you going to host events for others? Women? LGBT? Transgender?" she asked.

As I read through the list of different topics, I felt panic for a moment, but then I realized I'll cover those topics when I feel called, as I feel called. The creative process is a divine process, when I feel called to create an event or podcast episode, I trust that it's at the right time to really be in flow with the right people.

I responded to her, "The topic of men feels important to me at the moment, so I created an event for it."

Then she asked, "What are you going to do to make people feel safe at the event?"

This message might have spun me out in the past because I carry a limiting belief that "I'm responsible for other people's feelings and experiences. I don't particularly care if people like

170   COURAGE TO FIND PURPOSE

me. I just want them to feel safe." This deep desire for everyone in the world to feel safe and comfortable is a projection from my own lack of feeling safe, which is my deepest core wound and greatest lesson.

Of course I wanted everyone to feel safe at my events, yet with some new level of awareness, I could see that being asked what I was going to do to make others feel a certain way seemed unrealistic. As I've grown, I've learned that I'm not responsible for other people's experiences, even though I might wish I could control them.

I already did my best to arrive before the event, energetically set the space, and set the intention and guidelines. I did my best to facilitate conversation in a fair, reasonable way while still creating space to listen. I gave audience members a voice by allowing them to ask questions. If something intense came up during the event, I'd certainly do everything I could to support anyone that needed attention.

How people felt after that was not my responsibility; it was their own. I knew this woman asking the question wasn't asking from a genuine place because she was planning on attending; she was asking from a challenging place. I felt relieved knowing I could see this. It was one of those moments when I could really notice and feel grateful for my own growth.

I did my best to understand this person's world by sharing that I'd been sexually assaulted and creating these conversations seemed important to me. After a certain amount of back and forth within a message thread, I realized there was nothing I could say that would please her, nor any way I could connect. I felt like she'd already put me in the "bad" category, and I didn't feel like there was any way of getting out.

With that also came a deeper knowing that not everyone will like me and not everyone will get me.

. . .

One of the scariest things about writing this book is that some people may think it's shit, and they are right. It's also scary that other people will read it and believe it's amazing, and they're right too.

So as I finish writing, my doubts cause me to question: Should I add more stories? How vulnerably should I share about my past? Who should I include or not include in my book? Will people really get me or relate to these stories? Even recently, I contemplated scrapping it all together because that feels safer than opening myself up for judgement.

Although there are "best sellers" in the world, there's no perfect book everyone loves and enjoys. If I had the expectation of that happening, I'd set myself up for major disappointment, or worse, I might not even release the book at all.

What I told myself the other day is this: The best I can do is write my book for those who will benefit. If I thought about all the people that this wasn't for while I was writing, I'd write a boring book that was too general and I'd miss out on reaching my people.

I've learned time and time again, if I'm going to play big in this life, I'm going to be judged. But, really, I'm going to be judged anyway. I'm just going to be judged a bit more if I'm in the public eye.

When people see all the material I've put out into the world over the years, they say, "It's so easy for you to put yourself out there!"

I think back to the first video I uploaded and remember how many takes I did. I remember how many times I watched those takes and how much fear and shame I felt when I thought about others watching and judging it. Putting myself out there has never been easy. I've just been working that courage muscle for a long time.

Even now, when I think about people reading my book, I want to curl up in the fetal position or have my mom rock me like I'm a baby, but I know I'll still release it. And I know I'll write more books and release those too. And I know each time it'll get a little easier to allow myself to play big.

Being judged can be uncomfortable, yet knowing I'm holding my gifts back from the world is even more terrifying.

CHAPTER 14

I am enough

One day, I was sitting near a mom and her four-year-old daughter. This little girl had just put on a dress and was standing in front of the mirror. Swaying back and forth with a big smile on her face, she said, "Mommy, don't I look beautiful?"

Before the girl could finish the word beautiful, her mom snapped, "Modesty! It's your name to be modest. We don't say that."

I sat there shocked.

I was shocked, first off, that this little girl's name was "Modesty" and that she'll have to live not only with the name, but with the fear of being too boastful or confident for the rest of her days.

Secondly, I think what I witnessed will affect this little girl every time she looks in the mirror for the rest of her life.

My heart broke. I wanted to tell her that she did look beautiful and give her permission to be proud of herself and acknowledge her own beauty.

And, as much as I wanted to, could I really blame this mom? She was just teaching her daughter what she'd been taught. Her parents taught her what they were taught and so on.

I don't blame my parents for not teaching me how to love myself as a child; they don't know how to love themselves as adults. If you asked my mom, she would probably say that she thought I was a confident little kid and didn't need reinforcement, but that's far from true.

I remember singing in our Christmas performance in preschool when I was three years old. I was wearing a dress and flipped it up two times during the performance. Both times the crowd broke out in laughter.

After the performance, when we were reunited with our parents, I asked my mom, "Were people laughing at me?"

"Oh, they weren't laughing at you, honey. They were just laughing at what you did. You did something funny," she responded, like a good mother.

But since I wasn't trying to do anything funny, it felt like they were laughing AT me. As an adult I noticed that whenever laughter broke out around me, I would immediately think, "They must be laughing at me." It was a subconscious, automatic response, and it wasn't until this memory surfaced that my insecurity around people laughing made sense.

It's easy to see how we gather meaning to support our unworthiness from our experiences as children. We collect each of these small, yet traumatic experiences like playing cards and store them in our subconscious.

•   •   •

For most of my life, I thought I was pretty stupid.

When I was in elementary school, I remember the terror that filled my body when we took turns reading out loud. As soon as the teacher announced what we were doing, my anxiety would spike to severe levels and would only dip after I took my turn. I'm not sure if it was my anxiety, or the fact that pronouncing some words was difficult for me, or both but I dreaded it.

Studying was not my favorite as I had a hard time focusing, and I had to work at it longer to retain information. It seemed like my peers could study a little bit and ace the test. Not me. I had to put in many hours just to get a "decent grade" on a test.

To be honest, I never really got why grades mattered so much. For example, when I was in 3rd grade my mom was helping me study for a spelling test. After many practice rounds, it was clear I knew most of them and would probably get a B, which I thought was good enough.

"Mom, if I get a B, that's good enough."

"Don't you want to get them all right on the test?" she replied.

My mom didn't get it, and my parents and I would continue to have many conversations like this throughout my academic career.

I'll admit that cheating was one thing that got me through school. I know it's not something to brag about, and I'm not bragging. But it was an option that helped me get through the classes that were extra difficult for me to digest and retain. It wasn't my default. I would study and do homework, but it was a backup I used quite a bit.

I was in the "low" math classes with the students in the grade below me. Each day I walked into the class with so much fear and shame. I wished I were invisible. I would sneak into the desk in the back row and slouch down in my chair hoping to not draw any attention to myself. The truth is the most humiliating part of it all was that I still didn't understand the information. Unfortunately, you can't fake understanding algebra and you definitely can't copy off your neighbor's paper when you are supposed to show your work. Believe me, I tried. It probably won't come as a surprise when I say that my favorite classes were art and gym. THOSE were easy for me.

At the end of it though, I graduated high school with a C average, but I was also class president, student council president, peer helper secretary, and captain of all three of my sports teams—volleyball, basketball, and softball.

At this point in my life, I knew sports and leadership were my strengths, but I also thought I was pretty dumb. I mean, why else was school so much easier for those around me? The thought of going to college freaked me out. There was no way I could fit in there, but since my parents expected it of me, I'd have to somehow fake that too.

• • •

My parents "encouraged" me (read: "kind of forced me") to get a job when I was sixteen. My dad hooked me up with a job as a radiology intern clerk at the clinic where he worked. It was my responsibility to enter mammography results into the computer. I sat in a small room all by myself. I had zero inter-actions with humans and was bored as hell so I would often pull up a word document on my computer and journal about my life, love, and insights.

Even though they were only paying me $5.15/hr., which was

minimum wage at the time, I felt guilty for taking up company time by journaling on the clock. But I loved writing and I didn't like my job. Frankly, I didn't want to work my job at all.

When I brought up quitting to my dad, he said it wasn't an option, so I worked this job I hated until I was eighteen. I thought I was learning to be an adult, to do things I hated because I was obligated to do it. My parents said I was learning about responsibility.

When I was eighteen, I got a job cleaning the main areas of apartments for the elderly one day a week, a job my uncle hooked me up with. Some elderly people didn't like the quality of cleaning I did and I got fired from that job.

By this point, I'd determined I was lazy. No, I was stupid AND lazy. What job was I supposed to get now? I felt scared to grow up. If I couldn't handle these easy jobs, how was I supposed to support myself as an adult? Images of me living as a so-called "low-life" flashed before me.

• • •

Years later, I had started a business and found myself majorly struggling to focus on daily tasks. Out of curiosity, I set up an appointment to get tested for ADHD. After the first day of testing, the examiner looked at the test scores, then looked up at me and said, "You're in the right place."

What he meant was I "passed" with flying colors. . . or failing, depending on how you look at it.

I was so relieved. I didn't want to cop out and blame ADHD for every struggle in my life, but I will tell you it was freakin' validating to know I do indeed struggle to focus.

Because I hate tests, I was obviously not thrilled to keep going back each day for more testing. It's like saying, "Yes, you struggle with focusing on things. Now focus on this and I'll judge you on it." My insecurities from high school came rushing back, and there were many moments when I wanted to run out of the office and never come back. I still can't believe I was there of my own free will.

After a few test days he said he was surprised I went through as much schooling as I had with my attention problems.

I said, "I cheated a lot, or at least in grade school."

"But you made it work," he said, sounding encouraging. "You always find a way to make things work, don't you?"

A smile crept across my face. I never expected to be praised for cheating in my life. After all, we look down on it with shame, so this was a validating moment for me. I felt like he got me.

Even though I was there as an adult, I felt like a child finally getting the acceptance from an adult I'd been yearning for all of those years. I didn't think anyone else could really understand my world unless they were either me or they could jump inside my skin and walk around as me for a while or they were a professional psychologist looking at my test scores.

He said I tested on the low end of depositing information into my short-term memory if I don't know how to categorize it. Retaining information from boring-ass lectures on subjects I don't give a shit about (like algebra and biology) would be extremely difficult, even for a minute, because I had no categories to store it in.

He also acknowledged my emotional intelligence is extremely high, which at this point in my life I HAD figured out. I actually did really well on the IQ test too, which surprised me since, as you know, I'd never considered myself smart.

My strength is remembering and reading the feelings and patterns of people. This probably distracted me from actually listening and learning in classes and meetings. I was too busy reading the vibes among my fellow classmates or coworkers, tuned in to what was going on emotionally with them.

I could tell who has a crush on you and to what degree. I could tell who dislikes whom. I can tell who's distraught by their home life. I was also tuned in to the emotional state of my teacher or supervisor and if they are distracted during a lesson or presentation.

So, really, I'm not dumb. I just needed to figure out how my brain worked and where my default focus was set. Plus, a typical school setting isn't designed for most people, and I'm one of them.

This insight made me think back to all the kids I went to school with, and I wondered in what ways they thought they were stupid or not enough. I'm curious how they tried to "fake it," or fit in like I did. Many of them got better grades than me, but I excelled at sports when others didn't. Were we all believing we weren't enough?

• • •

Through the unfolding of understanding that I'm actually not stupid, I'm not lazy, and I'm more than enough just the way I am, I've also discovered my strengths.

I had always been intimidated by those people who always seemed to know what they were good at or what career they were drawn to. For most of my life, my gifts weren't obvious, yet now I can see they were right in front of me in the shape of things I love to do.

Like when I was younger, I pretended I had my own radio show, recording myself on my tape player. I fucking loved that tape player. I loved being the producer, bouncing back and forth from recording my favorite songs on the radio (mostly songs I'd requested) and recording myself as the show host.

Now I host a podcast, *Badass Spiritual Warriors*.

Around that same age, I loved to write lyrics that went with hip-hop beats in my head. At the time Salt-N-Pepa was my jam. (Ok, fine, they're still my jam.) I wrote and wrote and for a while I thought I'd be a musician. Later, writing actual music became extremely frustrating to me, which led me to believe I had no future in music, so I quit writing lyrics and fantasizing about being the next Salt-N-Pepa.

You can find some poetic, inspiring rhymes on my Facebook page and website.

I've always loved writing. In addition to being a writer for both my high school and college newspapers, I've consistently had a journal . (I mean, before I was ten, I think I called it a diary and actually wrote "Dear Diary" at the top of each entry.) Since those immature beginnings, I've written stories, poems, and rambled deep thoughts and desires.

Now. . . well, I wrote freaking a book, but you knew that already. And writing online content remains a big part of my work.

When I was in high school, I was always involved in planning things. As class president and student council president, I was in charge of organizing formal dances and homecoming weeks which meant using loads of creativity to decorate, plan skits, and organize everyone involved.

Since then, and on my own, I founded a wellness expo and created a spiritual summer camp for adults. I've hosted large-scale events for the city of Minneapolis and, honestly, I'm just getting started with events.

When it comes to public speaking, I started young.

Per my duties as class president, I gave a speech at graduation. The prospect scared me, but it also excited me a bit.

As an adult, I've been a presenter at festivals, expos, and conferences, and I plan to continue to give talks.

My first job working in the radiology department actually taught me one important lesson: I need to work WITH people. I cannot sit in a room alone.

So now I work directly in connection with people, and that's my favorite part of my work. I hire others to help me with the behind the scenes work, so I can focus on showing up fully for my people.

Like I mentioned before, I'm often highly alert to other people's experiences. In a classroom or meeting, this can distract me from learning and retaining information.

I've now come to see my ability to read a room as a superpower I use to authentically connect to my clients and the world. I believe this helps tremendously when I'm moving someone through their stuckness.

When I was young, I didn't always recognize my skills; other strengths I experienced as challenges. I didn't recognize the value of some of my interests. But they are all important parts of my path.

The key to connecting with my own intelligence and productivity was to understand my real interests and to do things my way. I dropped comparisons to other people's paths and I saw how significant mine was.

When I made these connections, I discovered I am more than enough just the way I am, and comparing myself to anyone around me won't make any sense, since we all have different strengths.

The journey of up-leveling my self-worth is never ending, and I'm so glad I can clearly see its importance and embrace it.

CHAPTER 15

Finding Purpose

The good thing about my life falling apart after my re-entry to the US was I had a clean slate and could create anything I wanted. I spent my evenings reading books on spirituality and business while brainstorming what I could do with my life. Instead of just looking at jobs, I wanted to create something that would make an impact on the world. For the first time, I felt like I was MEANT to create something big, I just wasn't sure what that was yet.

At first, I thought I wanted to get some sort of training in the health and wellness realm because that would help people. My mom had always shared the latest health information, and because I was doing my own physical healing, I had a vested interest. So I spent some time looking up certifications and degrees for acupuncture and nutrition because those were options

I was familiar with, but none of them felt right.

So I kept brainstorming about ways I could help people. I thought about how I went to Spain with zero language skills and left with intermediate skills, and that growth was all thanks to language-exchange partners I met up with while in Madrid.

I'd connected with them through a Spanish website similar to Craigslist, and we'd meet up in a coffee shop or park. We'd spend half the time speaking English and half the time speaking Spanish. Since I spoke English at work and most of my friends spoke English, it was nice to have rotating partners who helped me practice and improve.

I loved the idea of people connecting in person to practice languages. I discovered there were regional websites for this, but not a universal site someone could use anywhere in the world to find a language buddy, so I decided to create one.

I didn't know anything about creating a social-networking site, but I knew I was going to make it happen. I'm not sure if it was the confidence I got from living abroad, or if it was due to the fact that my world was falling apart, but I was being deliberate about how I built my world up this time around. The passion that fueled this project came from my desire to bring people together more than language improvement itself, although that's a fun result.

One thing I realized by traveling the world is that people are more similar than we think, and if I could bring people together to help each other out and learn each other's languages, that had to make a positive impact on the world.

For the first time in my life, I really felt purpose, so I invested the money I made from my corporate job into my language project. Often, I would work all night, writing language blogs, managing my team of programmers, and checking in with my designers. Working on my project seemed more exciting and fun than going out dancing, which was a huge shift for me. And since I'd quit drinking, I had so much energy to put into my passion project.

During the first year, I got over 25,000 members on my website, and I had an intern managing group language nights in Madrid, London, Cairo, Casablanca, Beijing, and Minneapolis. A local TV station did a story on my project, and I was interviewed on a local radio station. I made shit happen.

Unfortunately, the company that created my website from scratch didn't do a great job, and there were some glitches that appeared as members used my site (e.g., the birthday didn't update properly). I hired new developers, and they all said the same thing: "If I fix this, a new bug will show up somewhere else. It's going to be best to just start from scratch."

I had just poured my savings into creating the site, so I didn't have the money to invest in creating a new one. I was pretty devastated. Although I wanted to monetize the website, I felt like I needed to put that on hold until I made those changes. And I needed more resources to invest to make those changes so I felt pretty stuck.

While all of this was happening, as you know, I was starting a journey of self-discovery and had just learned my first healing modality. I had so much passion for the project of bringing people together to improve languages, yet I was also giving so much energy to my personal growth.

I started to feel like I was being pulled in two different directions, not knowing what I was supposed to be focusing my energy on and not clearly seeing my purpose. Should I invest more into my language website or put more into starting a healing business?

My purpose was about to become clearer.

• • •

While meditating one day, a couple of sentences lit up in front of me like neon lights. When I came out of the meditation, I couldn't exactly remember what those sentences were. Eyes?

Waking up? I couldn't quite remember, although whatever it was felt important.

The next day I grabbed a book I had just begun reading called *Merlin's Journal of Time: The Camelot Adventure* by Kara Starr and as I began to read the top of the page these words were left just waiting to be found: "There are those who carry sleeping in their minds a knowing. It is alas up to me to bring about their awakening."

Those words lit up on the page in front of me and it halted my reading. They took my breath away.

These words and the meaning they carried connected to a place in my soul that had been waiting to be reached.

Those were the words from my meditation. I had been asking for clarity about my purpose and now here it was, laid out clearly in front of me with no doubt in my mind.

I am meant to help people wake up to their inner knowing. I am meant to wipe the sleep from their eyes and to show them how to live their purpose.

I knew I could not know my purpose without living it. It wasn't a matter of if, it was a matter of when. I was certain of this, because even though I hadn't clearly known my purpose up until this point, I had already dedicated my life to find and live it. I was ready to move mountains.

My only question now was—How?

• • •

Just a couple days later, I felt another surge of energy course through my body and I urgently grabbed my journal and sat near the doorway of my room and began sketching out images and writing words and phrases. Everything flowed through me so quickly and intensely, I could barely keep up.

As the flow started to taper off, I sat in front of these pages that depicted myself writing books, teaching groups, and speaking.

I now saw what the grand vision looked like. I felt excitement—and fear.

Fear because how the hell could I do those things? Even though I had some deeper understanding of life at this point, I felt like I hadn't fully grasped many things. I felt like the spiritual teachings I received were only a partial view of how I could fully support someone to connect to their inner knowing and guide them to keep evolving. I still had so many questions and so much healing to do for myself.

I could confidently teach about meditation and intuition, but not really anything else. I still felt like a young child in the whole world of intentionally living my purpose.

So even though I could see and feel a grand vision, I was still brought back to the moment of looking at where my next steps would be. Just like I would if I were walking on rocks across the shallow water of the Mississippi near my house—I could only focus on where each foot would land next.

• • •

I decided to take the summer off from working on my language website, thinking I'd get more clarity on it in the future.

Since my priority was now on my own growth, I put my resources into that. I began to see a big transformation from one month to the next, which made me realize my past personal development had been so gradual before this. I started to see that everyone's development was pretty gradual unless they were intentionally putting in their effort to change it. I saw this as the difference between change and transformation. Change can be gradual and without effort while transformation is the immense change that happens with intention and effort.

It became strange to imagine that not that long ago, I didn't even know this world of higher self-awareness existed. Almost everyone looks at their lives through a lens of their own inner critic, but very few have the awareness that they can do something about it. I was finally seeing that there were ways to free me from my suffering.

I started a group for women who wanted to learn about spirituality and experience meditation. I was so nervous the first few times I hosted, yet the women who came loved it. It seemed natural for me to lead meditations and share themes on empowerment, so I kept hosting these events. I didn't charge anything for them at first, but I gained confidence in leading groups.

From there, I started teaching a few different classes that I did charge money for, and people enjoyed them and even referred their friends. This created more forward momentum for my mission, rolling into one-to-one sessions with clients, which was when I felt a rush of energy come through me.

"Doesn't it drain you to see clients?" a fellow healer asked me.

"Not at all, it actually gives me energy," I responded.

When I stood in front of a group of people or sat across from a client, I felt exhilarated. Although there have been a few times when I worked with someone who just wasn't a good fit and I did feel a little drained, this has been rare. Helping others evolve and heal has always brought me a deep sense of fulfillment.

• • •

So I had momentum in my healing and teaching mission, but I wasn't actually serving people full time so I decided to link up with a wedding officiant company in Minneapolis. My friend introduced me to the owner, and he was interested in having me on as a Spanish-speaking officiant. My Spanish skills were a little rusty since I hadn't been using them on a regular basis, but the idea of officiating someone's wedding was pretty exciting so I agreed. Before I knew it, I was officiating one to three weddings a week (in English and Spanish).

The first time I stood in front of a wedding audience, it was small, about ten people near the famous "Cherry and Spoon" statue in Minneapolis. Not going to lie, I was nervous. I made it through and received compliments when I finished.

I have to admit, though, I was scared of people perceiving me as too young for the job. I've always looked younger than I am, and I thought it might be a problem booking new weddings, since most officiants were much older than me.

For larger ceremonies, I usually met the couple in a coffee shop and went over the structure to see if we were a good fit. I met with one couple, and the first thing they said was, "Thank God! We thought you might be a really old guy."

I smiled and felt accepted. Every single couple I met wanted to work with me, which made me proud.

Standing in front of a room full of people, I practiced holding the space for a group and being the leader. Over the span of two years, I lead dozens of wedding ceremonies, and I felt grateful each and every time I was involved. I knew being an officiant wasn't ultimately part of my grand vision, but it was a stepping stone as I gained more confidence.

• • •

My next stepping stone was my attraction to big events. I loved attending expos and large events to explore anything related to spirituality, growth, and health. I met some pretty amazing people at them, so I decided I would create my own.

I chose to do it in Rochester with hopes of expanding it to other cities in Minnesota. Rochester is the home of Mayo Clinic, but it didn't have an event focused on healing beyond medicine. A college friend was also working at the main event facility there and encouraged me to make it happen.

I didn't have that many connections in Rochester, but I drove over an hour to the city every week to have meetings and knock on doors of businesses that I thought were a good fit for my event. I hustled hard the months leading up to it to line up speakers, activities, and partnerships, and to sign up vendor booths, which was where the bulk of the revenue was coming from.

Organizing this event gave me the opportunity to use skills I thought I had but hadn't had the chance to use. To say I gave it my all was an understatement.

"This is the most organized expo I've been to," said one expo attendee.

I proved to myself that I could indeed make it happen, which got me an event management position the following year for the Minneapolis Park Board. That led me to expand my network and learn even more about event management at events much larger than my own.

Since a health expo wasn't entirely aligned with my long-term vision of guiding others to live their lives with purpose, I decided it was time to move on and sold the event.

• • •

There were times I was frustrated that my purpose wasn't coming together more quickly. I could see it so clearly, yet it felt so far away. One flexible job I kept coming back to over the years was substitute teaching. It was a very non-committal job. I could choose the exact days I worked and sometimes only decided in the morning to go to work. Some months went by where I didn't work at all and some weeks I worked every day. I did this on and off for years as I took steps toward living my life with more purpose and intention.

Substitute teaching was easy on the days where I just had to push play on a video for seniors who didn't need to be babysat and difficult on days where the freshmen students' team effort was to make my life miserable.

"Is this what you want to do with your life? Be a substitute teacher?" one freshman girl asked one day as she rolled her eyes.

"No, it is not. But it is where I'm at," I replied.

The truth is, I was grateful for this non-committal job I could always come back to and so many days were really easy. I was often able to work on my own things as I watched the kids take a test or watch a movie.

But I was tired and yearned to be doing the thing I came here for. I felt like I had paid my dues and I had accumulated enough skills and confidence. Why the hell hadn't it all come together by now?

I'm not the most patient person and substitute teaching didn't exactly increase my patience. I felt the truth of my purpose and I wanted it to happen now. So although I didn't necessarily have a lot of patience, at least I could say that my deep sense of knowing demonstrated my faith. Although I was questioning *when*, I had no doubt in my mind of *if*.

Sure, I had moments of doubts and frustration, but it wasn't enough to take me down. I had been cultivating faith for years which meant I wasn't just drawing from my power, but a deeper sense of trust in who I am and my path ahead.

There is good reason why faith is often described as "unwavering," because when someone can cultivate faith, they have a strength so mighty nothing can shake it.

And I was starting to see not many people had this same sense of faith as I did.

Some time went by when I wasn't serving any clients at all. Some months, then closer to a year. I was still doing my work, but more casually. I think I just wanted a break from it all. I started to feel stuck and stifled. My anxiety started to creep back.

Then, I met a young gal who was interested in working with me. During our initial conversation, I just knew our relationship would be significant for both of us. I could feel my body vibrate in connection with her. I would help her with her anxiety by guiding her to live more in alignment with who she really was and she would help me live in alignment with who I really was, which in turn would help my anxiety that had started to creep back. See how this works?

"I feel anxiety the most intensely in my chest," she said. "I just feel like there's got to be more to life than just going through the motions. And I want to have more control over my life and the things I want to create."

I felt like she'd taken the words right out of the mouth of a younger version of myself. She was my perfect client.

Her entrance into my life changed something in me. It got me back in alignment with myself, my personal work, and my purpose. She helped me feel that my purpose isn't just about me; it's about all the people I need to be working with, and all the people they're supposed to be inspiring. I finally saw the truth: personal progression has a ripple effect.

When I first saw my purpose laid out in front of me, I felt like I wasn't ready to step into that role. Although I lacked confidence then, it was more than that. I felt like there were dots that needed to be connected. Finally, something really made sense with how I help people.

I had slowly released just doing energy healing. I embraced understanding all aspects of the human experience and evolution. I gained new skills and kept improving skills I had had along the way. But the thing I believe that has been equally beneficial to my clients is my fascination with human behavior.

I was part of many communities and I became a curious observer in them all. I noticed how some people seemed to be stuck while still being part of a supportive community. I noticed that although we can all relate to the typical aspects of growth, people also seemed to have very different avoidance strategies.

It also appeared to me that people could hang out in certain communities that felt better for these strategies, and in turn stop them from evolving, in spite of that being their purpose of being in said community.

My obsession with humans only grew as I saw every day as a new day to observe and learn from the world. I saw patterns. I saw some things that seemed interesting, yet I hadn't identified them yet. I stored all of this as data. I'm not the best at retaining information in my short=term memory and this is the reason why I struggled in school, yet when I'm fascinated by something, I have an incredible memory. I can remember exact words, conversations, and facial expressions of people very clearly.

I didn't understand how all of this would benefit my clients until I went into full investigation mode. It started to feel like part of my mission was to create my own theories about psychology, human behavior, and healing.

For me, it's not just about learning from a teacher or book, but taking in all information and then discerning the theories of my own. I feel exhilarated just writing this as I know I have important findings to share with the world and that it's all part of my mission.

The way I help people now is holistic. I like to look at things from all angles, from all aspects of self. I'm not just using one technique, because one technique doesn't work for everyone. I don't just want to give my clients short-term relief with the latest anxiety technique. I'm more interested in getting to the core and empowering them so they have lasting change in their lives. I'm more excited seeing the ripple effect of how my clients end up inspiring others to live their life with purpose.

• • •

If you would have told me when I was in college that my mission was to guide people out of stuckness into living a purpose-driven life, I wouldn't have even known what that meant. I needed to experience what I experienced to get to where I am now because none of it would have made any sense back then. I was finally shown the vision of my mission when I was able to grasp what that meant, and then I spent years working toward it.

When I wake up in the morning, I know I'm deeply connected to my path, and I feel like I'm a part of something big.

What I believe constitutes my purpose is the work I do to help humanity, the responsibility I take for my own life to evolve, and the presence I can access in a moment. I need all three of these to feel the fullness and richness of my life.

•   •   •

If you are a human in any form, you have experienced issues with your worthiness. It's part of the package deal of this human experience we are all in. Sometimes the inner critic is screaming in our head and other times it shows up as a stealth ninja directly from our subconscious, sabotaging our life in ways that elude our awareness.

Take a deep breath and know you are not alone in this and have some compassion for your fellow humans because they are also doing the best they can. Take a look at your life and see where you've let doubts keep you small, if you've given your excuses too much weight, or if you've given too much power to those around you. There is one thing I am certain of, and that is you have a unique purpose on this planet so grab your sword and keep stepping into your greatness. Even if the only thing you can see in front of you is the next place to step, trust that the rest will unfold with some faith, courage, and love.

What feels true to me is the importance of every single person stepping into their power at this time. Everyone is important and everyone's mission looks a bit different. Holding that back from the world could create that frustrating moment when the puzzle is almost finished, except for that one piece that belongs to you. It can also give the sense of relief and excitement when you slide that last piece into place.

Last Words

My first intention was to write a book that would inspire that younger version of myself, and in sharing it with the world, some others might find it to be a healing experience to read. As I wrote, it became clear that revisiting my past through this book was going to be a powerful step for my own growth and healing. And it has been. I've cried, forgiven, and accepted my past in ways I wasn't sure I needed to. So thank you for sharing this journey with me!

As you read this, I hope you found some interesting or entertaining stories. I hope some of you have also found some inspiration or taken lessons for your own life. If this has left you relating because you are deeply in the midst of anxiety, or feeling stuck, or just wanting to feel more purpose, please check out my training at www.janelleklander.com/freetraining. I know there will be some of you who are in alignment to do this work with me. And some of you will get some realizations from simply watching the video.

And lastly, if you want to connect, let's stay friends on Instagram or Facebook and post a photo of you and the book with #couragetofindpurpose and tag me, @janelleklander. If you aren't into that, just shoot me a DM. I'd love to hear from you. Seriously.

I believe in you and the path you were meant to lead. It's time to step into your greatness.

Love & Courage,

Janelle

www.janelleklander.com

This book was written in San Francisco,

Minneapolis, and Playa del Carmen.

Made in the USA
Monee, IL
18 September 2020